THE BOOK OF MY LIVES

ALSO BY ALEKSANDAR HEMON

The Question of Bruno

Nowhere Man

The Lazarus Project

Love and Obstacles

THE
BOOK
OF MY
LIVES

ALEKSANDAR HEMON

PICADOR

First published 2013 by Farrar, Straus and Giroux, New York

First published in Great Britain 2013 by Picador
an imprint of Pan Macmillan, a division of Macmillan Publishers Limited
Pan Macmillan, 20 New Wharf Road, London N1 9RR
Basingstoke and Oxford
Associated companies throughout the world
www.panmacmillan.com

ISBN 978-1-4472-1090-0

3 5 7 9 8 6 4 2

A CIP catalogue record for this book is available from the British Library.

Printed and bound by CPI Group (UK) Ltd, Croydon, CR0 4YY

Visit www.picador.com to read more about all our books
and to buy them. You will also find features, author interviews and
news of any author events, and you can sign up for e-newsletters
so that you're always first to hear about our new releases.

FOR ISABEL,

forever breathing on my chest

ACKNOWLEDGMENTS

■ ■ ■

I write fiction because I cannot not do it, but I have to be pressed into writing nonfiction. I'd like to thank the following people who pushed me to overcome my reticence and laziness: Slavenka Drakulić and Richard Swartz; John Freeman; Lee Froehlich; Sean Wilsey and the *McSweeney's* crew; David Remnick and, in particular, Deborah Treisman, whose intelligence, wisdom, and kind touch helped a few difficult pieces come into existence. My editor, Sean McDonald, the Tony Soprano of New York publishing, has been a loyal and supportive friend, and also made me rewrite when I didn't feel like it. My agent, Nicole Aragi, has by now become a de facto member of my family, so I normally express my gratitude to her by way of cooking—nevertheless, verbal gratitude is in order, as her patience, kindness, generosity, and a shockingly foul mouth have helped me through some very hard times. In addition to friendship and neighborly affection, Lana and Andy Wachowski provided me with a weeping office. My sister, Kristina, and my best friend, Velibor Božović Veba, have shared with me so much—not least their memories—that I can never thank them enough. My parents, Petar and Andja, have endured my childhood and adolescence and then lived to tell, becoming my friends and heroes in the process. Teri Boyd, my wife and partner, my forever and beyond, makes everything possible and endurable. Finally, my daughters, Ella, Isabel, and Esther, have graced all of my lives with love and meaning.

THE BOOK OF MY LIVES

THE LIVES OF OTHERS

■ ■ ■

I. WHO IS THAT?

On the evening of March 27, 1969, my father was in Lenin-grad, USSR, in pursuit of his advanced electrical engineer-ing degree. My mother was at home, in Sarajevo, deep in labor, attended to by a council of her women friends. She had her hands on her round belly, huffing and crying, but the council didn't seem too worried. I was orbiting around her, exactly four and a half years old, trying to hold her hand or sit in her lap, until I was sent to bed and ordered to sleep. I defied the order so as to monitor the developments through the (somewhat Freudian) keyhole. I was terrified, naturally, for even if I knew that there was a baby in her stomach, I still didn't know how exactly it was all going to work, what was going to happen to her, to us, to me. When she was eventually taken to the hospital in obvious and audible

pain, I was left behind with terror-provoking thoughts, which teta-Jozefina tried to counter with the guarantees that my mother would not die, that she would come back with a brother or sister for me. I did want my mother to come back; I did not want a brother or sister; I wanted everything to be the way it was, the way it already used to be. The world had harmoniously belonged to me; indeed, the world had pretty much been me.

But nothing has ever been—nor will it ever be—the way it used to be. A few days later, I was accompanied by a couple of adults (whose names and faces have sunk to the sandy bottom of an aging mind—all I know about them is that neither of them was my father, who was still in the USSR) to retrieve my mother from the hospital. One thing I remember: she was not half as happy to see me as I was to see her. On our way home, I shared the backseat with her and a bundle of stuff they claimed was alive—that was supposed to be my sister. The alleged sister's face was seriously crumpled, containing only an ugly, indefinable grimace. Moreover, her face was dark, as though she were soot-coated. When I traced my finger across her cheek, a pale line appeared under the soot. "She is filthy," I announced to the adults, but none of them acknowledged the problem. From thereon in, it would be hard for me to have my thoughts heard and my needs met. Also, chocolate would be hard to get.

Thus my sooty alleged sister's arrival marked the beginning of a tormentful, lonely period in my early development. Droves of people (bringing chocolate I couldn't touch) came to our home to lean over her and produce ridiculous sounds. Few of them cared about me, while the attention they paid to her was wholly, infuriatingly undeserved: she did nothing but sleep and cry and undergo frequent diaper changes. I, on the other hand, could already read small words, not to mention speak fluently, and I knew all kinds of interesting things: I could recognize flags of various countries; I could easily distinguish between wild and farm animals; cute pictures of me were all over our house. I had knowledge, I had ideas, I knew who I was. I was myself, a person, beloved by everyone.

For a while, as painful as her existence was to me, she was but a new thing, something you had to get around to get to Mother, like a new piece of furniture or a wilted plant in a large pot. But then I realized that she was going to stay and be a permanent obstacle, that Mother's love for me might never reach pre-sister levels. Not only did my new sister impinge upon what used to be my world, but she also obliviously asserted herself—despite having no self at all— into its very center. In our house, in my life, in my mother's life, every day, all the time, forever, she was there—the soot-skinned not-me, the other.

Therefore I tried to exterminate her as soon as an opportunity presented itself. One spring day, Mother stepped out of the kitchen to pick up the phone and left her alone with me. My father was still in Russia, and she was probably talking to him. Mother did stay out of my sight for a while, as I watched the little creature, her unreadable face, her absolute absence of thought or personality, her manifest insubstantiality, her unearned presence. So I started choking her, pressing my thumbs against her windpipe, as seen on television. She was soft and warm, alive, and I had her existence in my hands. I felt her tiny neck under my fingers, I was causing her pain, she was squirming for life. Suddenly, I recognized that I shouldn't be doing what I was doing, I shouldn't be killing her, because she was my little sister, because I loved her. But the body is always ahead of the thought and I kept up the pressure for another moment, until she started vomiting curdled breast milk. I was terrified with the possibility of losing her: her name was Kristina; I was her big brother; I wanted her to live so I could love her more. But, although I knew how I could end her life, I didn't know how I could stop her from dying.

My mother heard her desperate cries, dropped the phone, and ran to her aid. She picked my sister up, calmed her down, wiped off the curds, made her inhale and breathe, then demanded an explanation from me. My just-discovered love for my sister and the related feeling of guilt did not at all displace my self-protective instincts: I bold-facedly stated that she'd started crying and I'd merely put my hand over her mouth to prevent her from bothering Mother. Throughout my boyhood I always knew more and better than my parents thought I did—I was always a little older than what they could see. In this instance, I shamelessly claimed good intentions coupled with little-boy ignorance, and so I was warned and forgiven. There is no doubt I was monitored for a while, but I haven't tried to kill Kristina since, loving her uninterruptedly.

The recollection of that sororicide attempt is the earliest memory in which I can observe myself from outside: what I see is me *and* my sister. Never again would I be alone in the world, never again would I have it exclusively for myself. Never again would my selfhood be a sovereign territory devoid of the presence of others. Never again would I have all the chocolate for myself.

2. WHO ARE WE?

When I was growing up in Sarajevo in the early seventies, the dominant social concept among the kids was *raja*. If one had any friends at all, one had a *raja*, but normally the *raja* was defined by the part of town or the building complex one lived in—we spent most of our nonschool time playing in the streets. Each *raja* had a generational hierarchy. The *velika raja* were the older kids, whose responsibilities included protecting the *mala raja*—the smaller kids—from abuse or pocket-emptying by some other *raja*. The older kids' rights included unconditional obedience on the part of the *mala raja*, who could thus always be deployed to buy cigarettes, naked-lady magazines, beer, and condoms, or to volunteer their heads for the *velika raja*'s merciless filliping practice—my head was often submitted to a cannonade of the dreaded *mazzola*s. Many *raja*s were defined by and named after their leader, usually the strongest, toughest kid. We feared, for example, the *raja* of Ćiza, who was a well-known *jalijaš*, a street thug. Normally, Ćiza was old enough to be gainfully invested in various forms of petty crime, so we never saw him. He acquired a mythological quality, while his younger brother Zeko ran the daily operations of doing nothing in particular. It was he who we feared most.

My *raja* was a lesser, weak one, as we had no leader at all—all of our older boys, alas, took school seriously. We were defined by a playground between the two symmetrical, socialistically identical buildings in which we lived; we called it the Park. In the geopolitics of our neighborhood (known back then as Stara stanica—the Old Train Station) we were known as the Parkaši. The Park not only contained playground equipment—a slide, three swings, sandbox, merry-go-round—but there were benches as well, which served as goals whenever we played soccer. There were also, more important, the bushes where we had our *loga*—our base, the place where we could escape from Ćiza's marauding *raja*, where we hoarded things stolen from our parents or pilfered from other, feebler kids. The Park was therefore our rightful domain, our sovereign territory, on which no stranger, let alone a member of another *raja*, could trespass—any suspected foreigner was subject to preemptive frisking or punitive attack. Once we waged a successful campaign against a bunch of teenagers who mistakenly thought that our Park was a good place for smoking, drinking, and mutual fondling. We threw at them rocks and wet sand wrapped in paper, we charged collectively at the isolated ones, breaking long sticks against their legs as they helplessly swung their short arms. Occasionally, some other *raja* would try to invade and take control of the Park and we would fight a war— heads were cracked, bodies bruised, all and any of us risking a grievous injury. Only when Zeko and his troopers—our more powerful nemesis—came to the Park did we have to stand back and watch them swing on our swings, slide on our slide, piss in our sandbox, shit in our bushes. All we could do was imagine merciless revenge, deferred into an indefinite but certain future.

Now it seems to me that when I wasn't in school or reading books, I was involved in some collective project of my *raja*. Besides protecting the sovereignty of the Park and waging various wars, we spent time at one another's homes, swapped comic books and football stickers, sneaked together into the nearby movie theater (Kino Arena), searched for evidence of sexual activity in our parents' closets, and attended one another's birthday parties. My primary loyalty was to my *raja* and any other collective affiliation was entirely abstract and absurd. Yes, we were all Yugoslavs and Pioneers and we all loved socialism, our country, and its greatest son, our marshal Tito, but never would I have gone to war and taken blows for those. Our other identities— say, the ethnicity of any of us—were wholly irrelevant. To the extent we were aware of ethnic identity in one another, it was related to the old-fashioned customs practiced by our grown-ups, fundamentally unrelated to our daily operations, let alone our struggle against the oppression we suffered from Zeko and his cohorts.

One day I went, with nearly all of my *raja*, to Almir's birthday party. Almir was somewhat older than me, therefore an authority on many things I knew nothing about, including the explosive properties of asbestos, which we called "glass wool" and to which we somehow had unlimited access. On one occasion I had repeatedly ducked as he threw, like a hand grenade, a handful of "glass wool" wrapped in paper, promising an explosion that never came. Almir was also old enough to be getting into rock music, so at his party he played Bijelo Dugme, the Sarajevan rock band that was at the time scaring the living daylights out of our parents, what with their hairy looks and antisocial, antisocialist, asinine music. Other than that, Almir's was birthday business as usual: we ate the sandwiches, drank the juices, watched him blow out the candles on the cake, offered him our gifts.

For his birthday party, Almir was neatly dressed, which on that occasion meant a wool sweater with black and orange stripes, somewhat fluffy and comparatively resplendent— our socialist-Yugoslavia clothes were decidedly drab. The sweater visibly belonged to someplace else, so I asked him where it came from. It came from Turkey, he said. Whereupon I quipped: "So you are a Turk!" It was supposed to be a funny joke, but nobody laughed; what's worse, nobody thought it was a joke. My point was that a foreign sweater made him a kind of foreigner, a teasing possible only because it was manifestly and unquestionably untrue. The failed joke entirely changed the mood of the party: to my utter surprise Almir started inconsolably crying, while everyone looked at me admonishingly. I begged them to explain what it was that I'd said, and when they didn't, or couldn't, I tried to outline how the joke was supposed to have worked, digging thereby a deeper hole for myself. Let me not go through all the steps of the descent into a disaster—before long the party was over; everyone went home, and everyone knew that I had ruined it. That is, at least, how I guiltily remember it.

Subsequently, my parents explained to me that *Turk* was (and still is) a derogatory, racist word for a Bosnian Muslim. (Years later, I would recall my inadvertent insult, yet again, while watching the footage of Ratko Mladić speaking to a Serb camera upon entering Srebrenica, where he was to oversee the murder of eight thousand Bosnian Muslim men— "This is the latest victory in a five-hundred-year-long war against the Turks," he said.) After Almir's birthday party, I learned that a word such as *Turk* could hurt people. Moreover, it seemed that everyone knew about it before me. What I said *othered* Almir, it made him feel excluded from the group I was presumably unimpeachably part of, whatever group it was. Yet my joke was supposed to be about the flimsiness of difference—as we belonged to the same *raja*, having fought many a war together, the sweater established a momentary, evanescent difference. Almir was teasable exactly because there was no lasting, essential difference between us. But the moment you point at a difference, you enter, regardless of your age, an already existing system of differences, a network of identities, all of them ultimately arbitrary and unrelated to your intentions, none of them a matter of your choice. The moment you *other* someone, you *other* yourself. When I idiotically pointed at Almir's non-existent difference, I expelled myself from my *raja*.

Part of growing up is learning, unfortunately, to develop loyalties to abstractions: the state, the nation, the idea. You pledge allegiance; you love the leader. You have to be taught to recognize and care about differences, you have to be instructed who you *really* are; you have to learn how generations of dead people and their incomprehensible accomplishments made you the way you are; you have to define your loyalty to an abstraction-based herd that transcends your individuality. Hence the *raja* is hard to sustain as a social unit, your loyalty to it—to the "we" so concrete that I could (still) provide a list of names that constituted it—no longer acceptable as a serious commitment.

I cannot honestly claim that my insult was directly related to the fact that our wars and the golden days of our Park sovereignty ended soon thereafter. At some point all the conflicts with other *raja*s were resolved by playing soccer, which we were not all that good at. We still couldn't beat Zeko and his team, because they had the power to determine when a foul was committed or a goal scored. We did not dare touch them and even when we scored, the goal was always denied.

As for Almir, he didn't play soccer well enough and he got even more into Bijelo Dugme, a band I would forever hate. Soon he reached a point in his life when girls were accessible to him. He started leading a life different from our boyish lives, becoming someone other than ourselves well before we could. Now I don't know where he is or what happened to him. We no longer belong to "us."

3. US VERSUS THEM

In December 1993, my sister and parents arrived as refugees in Hamilton, Ontario. In the first couple of months, my parents attended English-language courses, while Kristina worked at Taco Bell, a purveyor of fast "ethnic" food, which she preferred to refer to as Taco Hell. Things were very complicated for them, what with the language my parents couldn't speak, the generic shock of displacement, and a cold climate that was extremely unfriendly to randomly warm human interactions. For my parents, finding a job was a frightening operation of major proportions, but Hamilton is a steel-mill town teeming with job-hungry immigrants, where many of the natives are first-generation Canadians and therefore friendly, and supportive of their new compatriots. Soon enough my parents did find work—Father at a steel mill, Mother as a superintendent in a large apartment building, in which many of the tenants were foreign-born.

Yet within months, my parents started cataloguing the

differences between us and them—*we* being Bosnians or ex-Yugoslavs, *they* being purely Canadian. That list of differences, theoretically endless, included items such as sour cream (our sour cream—*mileram*—was creamier and tastier than theirs); smiles (they smile, but don't really mean it); babies (they do not bundle up their babies in severe cold); wet hair (they go out with their hair wet, foolishly exposing themselves to the possibility of lethal brain inflammation); clothes (their clothes fall apart after you wash them a few times), et cetera. My parents, of course, were not the only ones obsessing over the differences. Indeed, their social life at the beginning of their Canadian residence largely consisted of meeting people from the old country and exchanging and discussing the perceived dissimilarities. Once I listened to a family friend in what could fairly be called astonishment as he outlined a substratum of differences proceeding from his observation that *we* like to simmer our food for a long time (*sarma*, cabbage rolls, being a perfect example), while *they* just dip it in extremely hot oil and cook it in a blink. Our simmering proclivities were reflective of our love of eating and, by extension and obviously, of our love of life. On the other hand, *they* didn't really know how to live, which pointed at the ultimate, transcendental difference—*we* had soul, and *they* were soulless. The fact that—even if the food-preparation analysis made any sense—*they* did not love committing atrocities either and that *we* were at the center of a brutal, bloody war, which under no circumstances could be construed as love of life, didn't at all trouble the good analyst.

Over time, my parents stopped compulsively examining the differences, perhaps because they simply ran out of examples. I'd like to think, however, it was because they were socially integrated, as the family expanded over the years with more immigration and subsequent marriages and procreation, so that we now included a significant number of native Canadians, in addition to all the naturalized ones. It has become harder to talk about *us* and *them* now that we have met and married some of them—the clarity and the significance of differences were always contingent upon the absence of contact and proportional to the mutual distance. You could theoritize Canadians only if you didn't interact with them, for then the vehicles of comparison were the ideal, abstract Canadians, the exact counterprojection of *us*. *They* were the not-us, *we* were the not-them.

The primary reason for this spontaneous theoretical differentiation was rooted in my parents' desire to feel at home, where you can be who you are because everyone else is at home, just like you. In a situation in which my parents felt displaced, and inferior to the Canadians, who were always already at home, constant comparison was a way to rhetorically equate ourselves with them. We could be equal because we could compare ourselves with them; we had a home too. Our ways were at least as good as theirs, if not even better—take our sour cream or the philosophical simmering of *sarma*. Not to mention that they could never get our jokes or that their jokes are not funny at all.

But my parents' instinctive self-legitimization could only be collective, because that was what they carried over from the old country, where the only way to be socially legitimate had been to belong to an identifiable collective—a greater, if more abstract, *raja*. Neither did it help that an alternative—say, defining and identifying yourself as a professor—was no longer available to them, since their distinguished careers disintegrated in the process of displacement.

The funny thing is that the need for collective self-legitimization fits snugly into the neoliberal fantasy of multiculturalism, which is nothing if not a dream of a lot of *others* living together, everybody happy to tolerate and learn. Differences are thus essentially required for the sense of belonging: as long as we know who we are and who we are not, *we* are as good as *they* are. In the multicultural world there are a lot of *them*, which ought not to be a problem as long as they stay within their cultural confines, loyal to their roots. There is no hierarchy of cultures, except as measured by the level of tolerance, which, incidentally, keeps Western democracies high above everyone else. And where the tolerance level is high, diversity can be celebrated and mind-expanding ethnic food can be explored and consumed (Welcome to Taco Hell!), garnished with the exotic purity of otherness. A nice American lady once earnestly told me: "It is *so neat* to be from other cultures," as though the "other cultures" were an Edenic archipelago in the Pacific, unspoiled by the troubles of advanced civilizations, home to many a soul-soothing spa. I had no heart to tell her that I was often painfully and sometimes happily complicated.

4. THAT'S ME

The situation of immigration leads to a kind of self-othering as well. Displacement results in a tenuous relationship with the past, with the self that used to exist and operate in a different place, where the qualities that constituted us were in no need of negotiation. Immigration is an ontological crisis because you are forced to negotiate the conditions of your selfhood under perpetually changing existential circumstances. The displaced person strives for narrative stability—here is my story!—by way of systematic nostalgia. My parents ceaselessly and favorably compared themselves with Canadians precisely because they felt inferior and ontologically shaky. It was a way for them to tell a true story of themselves, to themselves or anyone willing to listen.

At the same time, there is the inescapable reality of the self transformed by immigration—whoever we used to be, we are now split between *us-here* (say, in Canada) and *us-there* (say, in Bosnia). Because *we-here* still see the present *us* as consistent with the previous *us*, still living in Bosnia, we cannot help but see ourselves from the point of view of *us-there*. As far as their friends in Sarajevo are concerned, my parents, despite their strenuous efforts at differentiation, are at least partly Canadian, which they cannot help but be aware of. They have become Canadian and they can see that because they remained Bosnian all along.

The inescapable pressure of integration goes hand in hand with a vision of a life my parents could live if they *were* what they see as being Canadian. Every day, they see the Canadians living what in the parlance of displacement is called "normal life," which is fundamentally unavailable to them despite all the integrationist promises. They are much closer to it than any of *us* back home, so they can en-vision themselves living a normal Canadian life—my par-ents can experience themselves vicariously as the others, not least because they have spent so much time and mind on comparison with them. Still, they can never be *them*.

The best theoretical expostulation on the subject above is a Bosnian joke, which loses some of its punch in translation but retains an exceptional (and typical) clarity of thought:

Mujo left Bosnia and immigrated to the United States, to Chicago. He wrote regularly to Suljo, trying to convince him to visit him in America, but Suljo kept declining, reluc-tant to leave his friends and his *kafana* (a *kafana* is a coffee shop, bar, restaurant, or any other place where you can spend a lot of time doing nothing while consuming coffee or alcohol). After years of pressuring, Mujo finally convinces him to come. Suljo crosses the ocean and Mujo waits for him at the airport in a huge Cadillac.

"Whose car is this?" asks Suljo.

"It's mine, of course," Mujo says.

"That is a great car," Suljo says. "You've done well for yourself."

They get in the car and drive downtown and Mujo says: "See that building over there, a hundred floors high?"

"I see it," Suljo says.

"Well, that's my building."

"Nice," Suljo says.

"And see that bank on the ground floor?"

"I see it."

"That's my bank. When I need money I go there and just take as much as I want. And see the Rolls-Royce parked in front of it?"

"I see it."

"That's my Rolls-Royce. I have many banks and a Rolls-Royce parked in front of each of them."

"Congratulations," Suljo says. "That's very nice."

They drive out of the city to the suburbs, where houses have grand lawns and the streets are lined with old trees. Mujo points at a house, as big and white as a hospital.

"See that house? That's my house," Mujo says. "And see the pool, Olympic size, by the house? That's my pool. I swim there every morning."

There is a gorgeous, curvaceous woman sunbathing by the pool, and there are a boy and a girl happily swimming in it.

"See that woman? That's my wife. And those beautiful children are my children."

"Very nice," Suljo says. "But who is that brawny, suntanned young man massaging your wife and kissing her neck?"

"Well," Mujo says, "that's me."

5. WHO ARE THEY?

There is also a neoconservative approach to otherness: the others are fine and tolerable as long as they are not trying to join us illegally. If they are here already and legal at that, they will also need to adapt to our ways of life, the successful standards of which have long been established. The distance of the others from us is measured by their relation to our values, which are self-evident to us (but not to them). The others always remind us of who *we* truly are—we are not them and never will be, because we are naturally and culturally inclined toward the free market and democracy. Some of them want to be us—who wouldn't?—and might even become us, if *they* are wise enough to listen to what *we* tell them. And many of them hate us, just for the hell of it.

George W. Bush, in a speech to the faculty and students of an Iowa college in January 2000, succinctly summed up the neoconservative philosophy of otherness in his own inimitably idiotic, yet remarkably precise, way: "When I was coming up, it was a dangerous world and you knew exactly who they were. It was us versus them and it was clear who them was. Today, we are not so sure who the they are, but we know they're there."

And then *the they* flew in on September 11, 2001, and now *they* are everywhere, including the White House, by way of a falsified birth certificate. Every once in a while *we* round them up, take them to Guantánamo Bay on secret flights or arrest them in raids and deport them or demand from them to declare unequivocally that *they* are not *them*. And whoever *they* may be, *we* need to win the war against them so that we can triumphantly be alone in the world.

6. WHAT ARE YOU?

Here is a story I like to tell. I read it in a Canadian newspaper, but I have told it so many times that it occasionally feels as though I made it up.

A Canadian professor of political science went to Bosnia during the war. He was born somewhere in the former Yugoslavia, but his parents emigrated to Canada when he was a child, which is to say that he had a recognizably South Slavic name. In Bosnia, equipped with a Canadian passport and a UNPROFOR pass, he went around with armed, blue-helmeted escorts, fully protected from the war so he could study it. With his Canadian passport and a UNPROFOR pass, he passed through many checkpoints. But then he was stopped at one, and the curiosity of the soldiers was tickled by the incongruity of a South Slavic name in a Canadian passport, so they asked him: "What are you?" His adrenaline was no doubt high, he must've been pretty terrified and confused, so he said: "I am a professor." To the patriotic warriors at the checkpoint, his answer must've bespoken a childlike innocence, for they most certainly hadn't asked him about his profession. They must have laughed, or told stories about him after they let him go. He must have seemed unreal to them.

To be at all comprehensible as a unit of humanity to the ethnically brave men at the checkpoint he had to have a defined—indeed a self-evident—ethnic identification; the professor's ethnicity was the only relevant piece of information about him. What he knew or didn't know in the field of political science and pedagogy was hysterically irrelevant in that part of the world carved up by various, simultaneous systems of ethnic otherness—which, as a matter of fact, makes it not all that different from any other part of the world. The professor had to define himself in relation to some "other" but he couldn't think of any otherness at that moment.

To be a professor again he had to return to Canada, where he may have run into my parents, for whom he would have been a perfect specimen of one of them.

7. WHAT AM I?

My sister returned to Sarajevo after the war and worked there equipped with a Canadian passport. Because of the nature of her work as a political analyst, she encountered a lot of foreign and domestic politicians and officials. Brandishing a somewhat ethnically confusing name, speaking both Bosnian and English, she was hard to identify and was often asked, by both the locals and foreigners: "What are you?" Kristina is tough and cheeky (having survived an assassination attempt early in her life) so she would immediately ask back: "And why do you ask?" They asked, of course, because they needed to know what her ethnicity was so they could know what she was thinking, so they could determine which ethnic group she was truly representing, what her real agenda was. To them, she was irrelevant as a person, even more so as a woman, while her education or ability to think for herself could never overcome or transcend her ethnically defined modes of thought. She was hopelessly entangled in her roots, as it were.

The question was, obviously, deeply racist, so some of the culturally sensitive foreigners would initially be embarrassed by her counterquestion, but after some hesitation they would press on, while the locals would just press on without hesitation—my sister's knowledge, her very existence was unknowable until she ethnically declared herself. Finally, she would say: "I'm Bosnian," which is not an ethnicity, but one of her two citizenships—a deeply unsatisfying answer to the international bureaucrats of Bosnia, bravely manning government desks and expensive restaurants.

Instructed by my sister's experiences, when asked "What are you?" I am often tempted to answer proudly: "I'm a writer." Yet I seldom do, because it is not only pretentiously silly but also inaccurate—I feel I am a writer only at the time of writing. So I say I am complicated. I'd also like to add that I am nothing if not an entanglement of unanswerable questions, a cluster of others.

I'd like to say it might be too early to tell.

SOUND AND VISION

■ ■ ■

My father spent a couple of years in Zaire in the early eighties, constructing Kinshasa's electric grid, while Mother, Kristina, and I stayed at home in Sarajevo. In the summer of 1982, he came back home to take us to Zaire for a six-week vacation whose highlight would be a safari. I was seventeen, Kristina four years younger. We'd never been abroad, so we spent sleepless nights imagining everything we would experience that summer. The days, however, I spent watching the soccer World Cup, as I'd vetoed the possibility of going anywhere before the tournament was over. Once Yugoslavia was, as usual, eliminated early and embarrassingly, I became heavily invested in the Italian team. A couple of days before we left, I cheered for Italy in the World Cup finals, in which they beautifully beat Germany 3–1.

The World Cup over, we were on our way to Africa. The first stop was Italy, as we were supposed to catch an Air

Zaire flight to Kinshasa at Rome's Fiumicino Airport. At the airport we discovered that the flight had been canceled without explanation and until further notice. Father handled it all: he argued with the Air Zaire representatives; he retrieved our suitcases; he showed our passports to the Italian border-control officer. We were to wait for our flight at a hotel in a nearby town, to which we took a crowded shuttle.

Kristina and I were impatient to see what all the brouhaha over being abroad was about. What we saw during the shuttle ride was not all that impressive: nondescript buildings flying Italian flags; shop windows sporting pictures of the national soccer team, the Azzurri. Ever a great wrangler of silver linings, Father promised us that we would go to Rome, which was half an hour away by train, as soon as we had settled in at the hotel. He was our leader in this foreign world: he spoke in stern and bad English to the airport staff; he located the shuttle and got us on board; he exchanged money and dispensed it from his little manpurse with the confidence of a man used to international currencies. Kristina and I proudly bore witness to his negotiating two rooms for the Hemon family. He was conspicuously tall in his azure shirt, winking at us, entirely comfortable with all the worldly matters at hand.

But then, suddenly, dark fields of sweat appeared on his shirt, and he started frantically pacing the lobby. His manpurse was gone. He ran outside to see if he'd left it in the shuttle, but the shuttle, too, was gone. In garbled English, he yelled at the receptionist. He randomly interrogated guests and service staff who happened to enter the lobby. His shirt was now covered with sweat; he reeked of an imminent heart attack. Mother, who had previously idled in the lobby flipping a Rubik's cube, tried to calm him down. We still had the passports, she said; it was only our cash that had been stolen. (Coming from the promised land of socialism, we had no credit cards.) *Several thousand American dollars*, Kristina and I realized in horror. *All of our vacation money*.

Thus we found ourselves penniless in an obscure Italian town, unable to go to Rome for a day trip, let alone to Africa for a safari. The possibility of our simply giving up on being abroad and returning to Sarajevo was real and devastating. The hotel looked at a long wall, over which ugly, thirsty trees peeked at the displaced tourists. Father was on the hotel phone making calls, informing his co-workers in Zaire that we were stuck without money somewhere in Italy, hoping they could help him get the hell out of it, or find a way back to Sarajevo, or on to Zaire. In the process, he found out that the Kinshasa flight had been canceled because a Zairean army general had kicked the bucket and the dictator Mobutu had requisitioned all three Air Zaire intercontinental aircraft to fly his large entourage to the funeral.

The next day, Father was still obsessively analyzing every moment of the unfortunate trip from the airport to the reception desk, retracing his every step to determine at which point the clever thief struck, which would help identify him. Running out of clean shirts, he eventually came to the conclusion that the theft had taken place at the reception desk and reconstructed the full sequence of events: Father had put his manpurse down on the counter while filling out the forms, and, when he turned to wink at us, the receptionist had slipped it under the desk. Consequently, Father installed himself in the lobby, intently monitoring the receptionist—a handsome, innocent-looking young man—and waiting for him to make a revealing mistake.

Kristina and I had nothing to do. We listened to our Walkman, shareable because it had two outlets for earphones. We tried to watch television in our room, but even the movies were dubbed in Italian (although that afforded us a precious sight of John Wayne walking into a saloon full of bad guys and saying: "*Buon giorno!*"). We wandered around the nameless town, excited, in spite of everything, to be experiencing the world: there was the vague smell of the Mediterranean, as if the town were on the sea; the lush variety of design in the pasta store around the corner; the intense redness of the tomatoes and the din of bartering at the local market; shops packed with the things that socialist teenagers coveted (rock music, denim clothing, gelato); taverns full of loud men watching replays of the World Cup games and reliving the triumph. (I wanted to watch the finals all over again, to see Marco Tardelli screaming in celebration after scoring the second goal, but Kristina objected.) When everything shut down for the noon siesta, we trailed a group of suntanned young people, assuming that their final destination was fun, until we ended up on an entirely unanticipated beach. It turned out the town was called Ostia and that it was, in fact, on the coast.

Returning from our expedition, eager to deliver the good news, Kristina and I found Father sweating like a hysterical hog and glaring at the receptionist from a far corner of the lobby—a veritable self-appointed hotel detective. Even after a couple of shifts on the watch, he'd failed to catch the suspect in another act of stealing or to collect any evidence against him. From where we stood, his aura of leadership was sadly diminished. When we announced that we'd discovered salt water, Mother finally abandoned her Rubik's cube and took charge.

First, we went with her to a jewelry store we came upon around the corner, where she sold her favorite gold necklace after a hard bargain. Then she distributed the money; Father, for obvious reasons, did not get any at that time. Kristina and I instantly went to the music store where we'd already browsed; we pooled our money to buy a cassette tape of David Bowie's *Low*. When we came back with our treasure, Mother informed us that we were required to participate in an evening family walk. I still cherish the memory, which fully contains all the smells, sounds, and visions from the evening when the Hemons leisurely strolled along the Lido, *as if on vacation*, the parents holding hands, *as if in love*, the children licking gelato paid for with family gold. In the middle of a catastrophe, the Hemons managed to scrounge up some makeshift joy.

The following day Father told us that we would fly to Brussels, where we could catch an evening flight to Kinshasa—the general buried, Mobutu had released the aircraft. As we left the hotel, Father shot one last glance of sublime hatred at the receptionist, but Kristina and I were strangely sad to be leaving. On a building across the street from the hotel, a passionate soccer *tifoso* had draped a vast flag, the same shade of blue as my father's sweat-stained shirt, which read "*Grazie, Azzurri.*"

We spent a day in Brussels, admiring resplendent duty-free shops and spotless bathrooms. In the evening, we were finally on the flight to Africa. Attached at the Walkman, Kristina and I listened to Bowie's beautiful album. Flying along the dividing line between night and sunset, on one side we could see complete darkness and on the other a horizon in spectacular flames. In Ostia, something had awoken in us and *Low* was the soundtrack for what we were, changed, experiencing. That night, we could not sleep at all, flipping the cassette back and forth, until the batteries ran out. "Don't you wonder sometimes," sang Bowie all the way to Kinshasa, "about sound and vision?"

FAMILY DINING

■ ■ ■

I

Back in the happy days of my mildly troubled adolescence, my parents returned from work around 3:45 p.m., so the family dinner—which we called *ručak*, which is lunch—was at 4:00. The radio would always be on for the four o'clock news, featuring all varieties of global decline, international disasters, and the homey accomplishments of socialism. My sister and I would submit to an interrogation on school matters by our parents and were never allowed to eat in silence, let alone read or watch television. Whatever conversation we mustered up had to be terminated for the weather forecast at 4:25; the dinner was usually over by 4:30. We were obligated to finish everything on our plates and thank our mother for her efforts. Then everyone would retreat for a nap, after which we would have coffee and cake, sometimes an argument.

My sister and I took our family meals to be a means of parental oppression. We regularly complained: the soup too salty, the green peas served too often, the weather forecasters obviously lying; the cake too unattractive. For the two of us, the ideal dining experience simultaneously involved *ćevapi* (grilled skinless sausages, a kind of Bosnian fast food), comic books, loud music, television, and the absence of our parents and weather forecasting.

In October 1983, at the age of nineteen, I was conscripted in the Yugoslav People's Army and served in Štip, a town in eastern Macedonia, which apart from the military barracks was home to a bubble-gum factory. I was in infantry, where the dominant training approach was ceaseless debasement, beginning with the way we were fed. At mealtime, we would line up on a vast tarmac—where our hunger was exacerbated by the bubble-gum smells wafting in the air—undergo a roll call, and then march into the cafeteria, unit by unit, soldier by soldier, sliding our icky trays along the rails, each of us thinking up a way to solicit a bigger slice of bread from the all-powerful and pitiless kitchen staff.

The choices were impressively limited, stamping upon our minds the basic quality of *serving*—none of the choices could ever be ours. For breakfast, apart from dry bread, we would get a boiled egg, a packet of rancid margarine, occasionally a slice of sticky, thick, unsmoked bacon (if you were deft and quick, which I was not, you could solicit it from a Muslim); we washed it all down with tepid, sweet tea or decondensed milk in plastic cups that had been absorbing grease for an eternity. Lunch always required the use of a spoon; the most common and widely beloved dish (which I profoundly hated) was a thick bean soup—complete with tiny sprouts that looked exactly like maggots—because it filled up the starving heroes-in-the-making and allowed for an encyclopedia of fart jokes, complete with sound effects. Dinner consisted of modified lunch leftovers, unless it was the very same lunch all over again (once we had green peas for nine consecutive meals), plus a greasy cup of prune-based bowel-movement potion. Even if we wanted to talk to one another, there was never time for conversation, for we had to devour the crappy grub quickly and then clear out for another ravenous unit. A persistent rumor claimed that bromide was added to all the food to keep soldiers docile and hard-ons down.

And those were the good meals. We longed for them when we left the barracks to be deployed in the arid Macedonian plains and practice sacrificing our lives to dam the flood of foreign invasion. Between hypothetical heroic victories we slurped indefinable concoctions out of canteens or munched on the contents of our MREs: stale crackers, ancient tuna from cans, impenetrable dried fruit. Perpetually hungry, I recalled my family dinners before sleep and constructed elaborate future menus featuring roast lamb or ham-and-cheese crepes or my mother's spinach pie. The fantasy just made me hungrier and more despondent.

Apart from the continuous roughing-up that was to induce us into the deprivations of manhood, the army was supposed to be one big family, a manly community bound by loyalty and comradeship, sharing everything. As a matter of fact, at no time did we practice anything even close to sharing, unless you count the farts. You never, ever offered to anybody your goodie-laden package sent from home nor did you leave any food in your locker, which you were forbidden to lock—at the Yugoslav People's Army's barracks, pilfering was already being rehearsed for the future wars. If you had any food left after stuffing yourself, you bartered it for clean socks and shirts, for an extra shower or a daytime fire-watch shift. Food wasn't meant to be shared, because it was a survival commodity. I had no trouble imagining heroically facing the foreign enemy only to get a bullet in my back and die for the tuna can in my pocket.

The only one who willingly shared his food was the soldier in my unit who soon after his arrival went on hunger strike because he didn't want to serve. Our superior officers ignored his self-famishment, certain he was bluffing. But he was quickly fading and soon it was clear to all of us he was dead serious, willing to go all the way. But the officers spent their days being idiotically certain they could see through his devious ploy, and the starving soldier, however weak, had to be present for the roll call and the subsequent meal. So a couple of fellow soldiers were always required to help him stay on his feet in the lineup and then totter to the cafeteria. Suddenly he acquired a lot of great comrades, all of whom were determined not to let his allotment of food go to waste. Eager to get his food, his escorts would fight over his boiled egg, piece of bread, or bowl of beans, while he smiled with his eyes closed, his emaciated cheek laid on the table. Perhaps he was delirious, but I thought he may well have been envisioning dinner at home with his family. A few days later, he was gone, and I never found out what happened to him. I hope he went back home, wherever it may have been.

A few months after my conscription, my mother and sister undertook a two-day trip from Sarajevo to visit me for a weekend. At the time, I was deployed in Kičevo, in western Macedonia, for truck-driver training. The weather lived up to a dismal forecast, so we spent the two days in a dismal hotel. Mother had dragged heavy bags of food on the many trains from Sarajevo and brought along a feast: veal schnitzels, fried chicken, spinach pie, even a custard cake. She spread a towel on the bed, as there was no table, and I ate from food containers, much of it with my fingers. The first bite into the spinach pie brought tears to my eyes and I silently swore that from thereon in I'd always respect the sanctity of our family meals. I wouldn't entirely keep my promise, needless to say, but as the perfectly mixed spinach and eggs and cheese and filo dough melted in my mouth, I felt all the love that could be felt by a boy of nineteen.

2

An eventful century or so ago, my paternal ancestors left behind what was then Galicia, the easternmost province of the Austro-Hungarian Empire (now western Ukraine), and resettled in Bosnia, which had recently been annexed to the Habsburg domain. My peasant foreparents brought with them a few beehives, an iron plow, many songs about leaving home, and a recipe for perfect borscht, a dish previously unknown in that part of the world.

There was no written document, of course; they carried the recipe within themselves, like a song you learn by singing it. In the summers of my childhood, which I spent at my grandparents' house in the countryside of northwest Bosnia, a committee of aunts (sometimes actually singing a song) would start early in the morning, chopping various vegetables, beets included, then, under my grandmother's supervision, boiling them mercilessly on a woodstove in the infernally hot kitchen. The Hemon borscht contained whatever vegetables were available in the garden at the time—onions, cabbage, peppers, pole and other beans, even potatoes—plus at least one kind of meat (though, for some reason, never chicken), all of which was purpled by the beets to the point of being unidentifiable. I've discovered that no one in my family knows exactly what should go into borscht, though there is a consensus that it must contain beets, dill, and vinegar. The amounts and proportions change with the cook, just as a song changes with the singer. As far as I can tell, it never bothered any Hemon that there was always at least one mystery ingredient in the borscht on the table. (Carrot? Turnip? Peas?) Whatever the variation, no bad borscht was produced. The vinegary tartness, always refreshing in the summer; the crunchy beet cubes (beets go in last); the luck-of-the-spoon-draw combinations of ingredients, providing different shades of taste with each slurp—eating borscht was always eventful, never boring.

I can still see my grandmother, the senior borscht cook, with an enormous, steaming pot in her hands, wobbling from the kitchen out to the yard, sweat drops sliding off her forehead and into the borscht for that special final touch. She'd deposit the pot on a long wooden table, where the Hemon tribe was waiting, aflutter with hunger. Then it would be ladled out, with at least one piece of meat distributed to each of the mismatched bowls on the table. There were often so many of us that we had to eat in shifts; one summer, my sister and I counted forty-seven people at my grandparents' for lunch, most of them related to us. Among the Hemons, the intensity of the slurping is proportional to the enjoyment of food, and the borscht that day yielded a symphony.

Festive though it may have been, the country version of the Hemon family lunch was not a ceremonious meal. Served in the middle of a workday, lunch was supposed to provide nourishment and reprieve for those who had worked the fields in the sun and would return to work until sunset. Thus, whatever we ate had to be simple and abundant, and borscht fit the requirements perfectly. Like all the dishes that are traditional in my family—pierogi/*vareniky*, which are, really, potato ravioli, or *steranka*, dough boiled in milk, the very mention of which brings tears to my father's eyes—borscht is poor people's food. It was designed (if indeed it was ever designed, rather than just randomly concocted) not to delight the sophisticated senses but to ensure survival. Anything ingested by spoon is close to the top of the survival-food pyramid on which my family bases their nutrition, and borscht is, without a doubt, the spooniest dish there is. (The point of sushi shall remain puzzling to generations of Hemons to come.) Borscht must be cooked in a large pot, it must feed a large number of people, and it ought to last well beyond one meal. (I don't remember us ever running out of borscht; the pot was always magically bottomless.) It is an essential leftover dish, always better the next day. It is definitely not something to be cooked for two people; you do not meet a friend over borscht, let alone share it with a date by romantic candlelight, even if you are able to suppress the slurping urge. There is no wine that matches it. A perfect borscht is a utopian dish: ideally, it contains *everything*; it is produced and consumed collectively; and it can be refrigerated and reheated in perpetuity. A perfect borscht is what a life should be but never is.

In the early, lonely days of my life in Chicago, I often struggled to reproduce the pleasures of my previous existence in Bosnia. I nostalgically sought good—I didn't expect perfect—borscht. But what I found at Ukrainian restaurants or in supermarkets with ethnic-food shelves was merely thin beet soup, and I was forced to try to reconstruct the family borscht from my addled memory. I'd make a pot for myself and live on it for a week or two. But what I made in this land of sad abundance was nowhere near what I remembered. I was always missing at least one ingredient, not counting the mystery one. More important, there is nothing as pathetic as solitary borscht. Making borscht for myself helped me grasp the metaphysics of family meals—the food needs to be prepared on the low but steady fire of love and consumed in a ritual of indelible togetherness. The crucial ingredient of the perfect borscht is a large, hungry family.

THE KAUDERS CASE

■ ■ ■

I. VOLENS-NOLENS

I became friends with Isidora when I was in college, at the University of Sarajevo, in 1985. We had both transferred to General Literature: she from Philosophy, I from Engineering. We met in the back of our Marxism class. The Marxism professor had his hair dyed hell-black, and had spent time in mental institutions. He liked to pontificate about man's position in the universe: man was like an ant holding on to a straw in a biblical flood, he said, and we were too young to even begin to comprehend how dire our metaphysical situation was. Isidora and I bonded over tear-inducing boredom.

Isidora's father was a well-known chess author, good friends with many a famous grandmaster, including Fischer, Korchnoi, and Tal. He reported from world-championship matches and wrote a large number of books about chess; the most famous one was for beginners: the *Chess Textbook* (*Šahovska čitanka*), essential for every chess-loving household, including ours. Sometimes when I visited Isidora, she would be helping her father with correcting the proofs. It was a tedious job of reading back transcripts of chess games to each other (Ke4 Rd5; c8=Q b7; et cetera), so they would occasionally sing the games, as if performing in a chess musical. Isidora was a licensed chess monitor, and she traveled the world with her father, attending tournaments. She would come back with stories about all the strange people she had met, as chess attracts all kinds of characters. Once in London, she told me, she'd met a Russian immigrant named Vladimir, who claimed that Kandinsky had merely been a Red Army officer running a workshop of anonymous artists and then appropriating their paintings as his own. True or not, the story implied that the world was a terribly interesting place, where there was more than met the eye even in Kandinsky.

We were bored in Sarajevo; it was hard not to be. We had ideas and plans and hopes so big, we thought, they could change the small-city staleness, and ultimately the world. We always undertook unfinishable projects and never finished them: once we started translating from English a book on the Bauhaus, but quit after the first paragraph; then a book on Hieronymus Bosch, but never reached the second page— our English was not very good at all, and we had neither good dictionaries nor much patience. We read about and discussed the artists of Russian Futurism and Constructivism, and we were attracted to the revolutionary possibilities of art. Isidora was constantly thinking up performances in which, for instance, we would show up somewhere at the crack of dawn with a hundred loaves of bread, and make crosses out of them. It had something to do with the dawn of the new era and Khlebnikov, the poet, as the root of his name, *hleb*, was the common word for bread in many Slavic languages. We never did it, of course—just showing up at dawn was a sufficient obstacle. On the steps of the People's Theater in Sarajevo, she staged a performance based on *The Mountain Wreath*, the classic Serbian epic poem, featuring a few of her friends (though I didn't take part) who were less worried about the subversive messages of the performance than about the possibility of the random passersby heckling them in that particularly menacing Sarajevan way.

Eventually, we found a way to act upon some of our revolutionary fantasies within a socialist youth institution, which gave us a space, ensured that we had no interest in getting paid, and made clear that we were not to overstep the borders of decent public behavior and respect for the values of socialist self-management. A few more friends joined us (Guša, living in London now; Goga—Philadelphia; Bucko—Sarajevo). We adorned the space with slogans hand-painted on bedsheets sewn together: "The fifth dimension is being created!" was one of them, straight from a Russian Futurist manifesto. There was an anarchy sign and a peace sign (a concession to the socialist-youth people) and Kasimir Malevich crosses, although we had to repaint some of them, because, in the blurry eyes of the socialist-youth hippies, they alluded to religion. This thing of ours was called Club Volens-Nolens, a ludicrously pretentious name.

We hated pretentiousness; it was a form of self-hatred. Planning the opening night, we had fierce discussions over whether to invite the Sarajevo cultural elite, the idle people who attended all the openings, and whose *cultureness* was largely conveyed by wearing cheap Italian clothes bought in Trieste or from the shady guys on the streets pushing contraband. One idea was to invite them, but to have barbed wire all over the place, so their Italian clothes would be subversively ripped. Even better, we could do the whole opening in complete darkness, except for a few stray dogs with flashlights attached to their heads. It would be fabulous, we agreed, if the dogs started biting the guests. But we realized that the socialist hippies would never go for that, as they had to invite some socialist elite to the opening in order to justify the whole project. We settled for inviting a few local thugs along with the elite, hoping that fights might break out, bloodying an upturned nose or two.

Alas, it was not to happen. No dogs, no bites, no fights— the opening was attended by a lot of people, who all looked good and behaved nicely. Thereafter we had programs every Friday. One Friday, there was a panel discussion on alcoholism and literature with all the panelists drunk, and the moderator the drunkest of all. For another Friday program, two comic-book artists came from Serbia to speak about their art and show their work in an exhibit. One of them got terribly drunk and stage-frightened, so he locked himself in the bathroom, refusing to come out. The audience waited while we begged him to open the stall. Eventually, he collected himself, left the security of the bathroom, and got on the stage, from which he hollered at the audience: "People! What is wrong with you? Do not be fooled by this. This is bullshit!" We loved it. Then there was the time when we showed a film called *Rani radovi* (The Early Works), suppressed in Yugoslavia because it belonged to the film movement from the sixties known as the Black Wave, which painted a not-so-rosy picture of socialism. It had never been shown in Sarajevo and we all wanted to see it, so we found a copy, rented a projector, and brought in the director from Belgrade, who was flattered by the invitation from a band of fawning young enthusiasts. The film was heavily influenced by Godard: young people walked around junkyards discussing comic books and revolution, and then made out with mannequins, those immortal symbols of consumerist alienation. The projectionist, conditioned by the soft demands of soft porn, switched the reels and showed them out of order. Nobody noticed except the director, who was tipsy and excited that his film was being shown at all. We organized a performance of John Cage's music, the first (and possibly the only) one ever in Sarajevo: we played records with a composition performed by twelve simultaneously screeching radios, and the infamous "4:33"—a stretch of silence on the record which was supposed to provide the time for the audience to create its own inadvertent, incidental music. The audience, however, consisting by this time mainly of the idle elite, didn't notice that "4:33" was playing at all, didn't give a diddly fuck about the music it was itself producing, and was, instead, getting happily drunk. Then the performer, who had traveled to Sarajevo forgoing a family vacation at the peril of divorce, stepped in front of the microphone. The few audience members who glanced at the stage saw a hairy man eating an orange and a banana in front of the microphone, performing, unbeknown to almost everyone present, the John Cage composition appropriately titled "An Orange and a Banana."

It was irritating not to be irritating to the elite, so even on the nights when we just spun records, the goal was to inflict pain: Guša, the DJ, played Frank Zappa, Yoko Ono screaming in dissonance, and Einstürzende Neubauten, the fine German musicians who liked to use chain saws and power drills to produce music. The elite was undeterred, though it shrank in numbers—we wanted them to be there so as to experience severe mental pain. This concept did not fly too well with the socialist hippies.

The demise of Club Volens-Nolens (which means "willy-nilly" in Latin) was due to what is usually called "internal differences"—some of us thought we had made too many compromises: the slide down the slippery slope of bourgeois mediocrity (the socialist version) had clearly begun when we gave up the stray dogs with flashlights. Before we called it all off, we contemplated having stray dogs, this time rabid, for the closing night. But Club Volens-Nolens went out with a whimper, rather than a mad bark.

After the demise, we sank back into general ennui. I busily wrote self-pitying poetry, eventually accumulating about one thousand dreadful poems, the subject of which flip-flopped between boredom and meaninglessness, with a dash of hallucinatory images of death and suicide. Like many young people raised in the comforts of socialism, I was a nihilist and living with my parents. I even started thinking up an Anthology of Irrelevant Poetry, sensing that it was my only hope of ever getting anthologized. Isidora was willing to do it, but nothing came of it, although there was a world of irrelevant poetry everywhere around us. There was nothing to do, and we were quickly running out of ways to do it.

2. THE BIRTHDAY PARTY

Isidora's twentieth birthday was coming up, and she—ever disinclined to do it the normal way—did not want it to have the canapés-booze-somebody-fucking-in-the-bathroom format. She thought that it should have the form of an art performance. She couldn't decide whether it should be modeled on a "Fourrieristic orgy" (the idea I favored) or a Nazi cocktail reception, the template for which could be found in the patriotically proper movies of socialist Yugoslavia: the Germans, all haughty, decadent bastards in impeccable uniforms, throwing a lavish party, in 1943 or so, while local whores and "domestic traitors" lick their tall, shining boots, except for a young Communist spy who has managed to infiltrate the inner circle and who will make them pay in the end. For some unfortunate reason, the orgy lost out to the Nazi party.

The birthday party took place on December 13, 1986. The young men donned black shirts and had oil in their hair. The young women wore dresses that reasonably approximated gowns, except for my teenage sister, who was cast as a young Communist girl, so she wore a girly Communist dress. The party was supposed to be taking place sometime in the early forties, right after the beginning of the German occupation. The narrative featured all the implicit decadence seen in the movies, and then some pseudo-nihilistic whimsy. There were mayo swastikas on the canapés; there was a sign on the wall saying "In Cock We Trust"; there was a ritual burning of Nietzsche's *Ecce Homo* in the toilet; my sister was detained as a young Communist in one of the rooms, designated as a makeshift prison; Guša and I fought over a bullwhip; Veba (who lives in Montreal now) and I sang pretty, sad Communist songs about fallen strikers, which we liked to do at every party; I drank vodka out of a cup and wore tall boots, as I was cast as a Ukrainian collaborator. In the kitchen (you can always find me in the kitchen at parties) we discussed the abolishment of the Tito cult and the related state rituals, still running strong. We entertained the idea of organizing demonstrations: I would be looking forward, I said, to smashing some store windows, as some of them were ugly and I liked glass shards. There were people at the party and in the kitchen whom I didn't know, and they listened very carefully. The morning after, I woke up with a sense of shame that always goes with getting too drunk, usually remedied by a lot of citric acid and sleep. Yet the sense of shame wouldn't go away for a while. Indeed, it is still around.

The following week I was cordially invited over the phone to visit the State Security offices—a kind of invitation you cannot decline. They interrogated me for thirteen hours straight, in the course of which I discovered that all the other people who attended the party had visited or were going to visit the warm State Security offices. Let me not bore you with the details—let's just say that the good cop, bad cop routine is a transcultural cliché, that both of the cops knew everything (the kitchen listeners listened well), and that they had a big, very big problem with the Nazi cocktail reception framework. Naïvely, I assumed that if I explained to them that it was really just a performance, a bad joke at worst, and if I elided the kitchen demonstration fantasies, they would just slap our wrists, tell our parents to whup our asses, and let us go home, to our comfy nihilistic quarters. The "good" cop solicited my opinion on the rise of fascism among the youth of Yugoslavia. I had no idea what he was talking about, but I strenuously objected to such tendencies. He didn't seem too convinced. As I was sick with flu, I frequently went to the bathroom—no keys on the inside, bars on the window—while the good cop was waiting outside, lest I cut my wrist or bang my head on the toilet bowl. I looked at myself in the mirror (which I could have broken to slit my throat) and thought: "Look at this dim, pimply face, the woozy eyes—who can possibly think I am dangerous, let alone a Nazi?" They let us all go, eventually, our wrists swollen from slapping. My mother was out of town visiting family, my father was in Ethiopia ("We send him to Ethiopia," the bad cop said to me, "and this is how you thank us?"), and I refrained from informing them that I had been detained by State Security, thinking it would all just go away.

But away it did not go. A few weeks later, the Sarajevo correspondent of the Belgrade daily *Politika*—which was on its way to becoming the hysterical nationalist voice of the Slobodan Milošević regime—received an anonymous letter describing a birthday party at the residence of a prominent Sarajevo family, where Nazi symbols were exhibited and values belonging to the darkest recesses of history were extolled in violation of everything our society held sacred. Rumors started spreading around Sarajevo, the world capital of gossip, speculating about who might have been at the party and at whose home it had taken place. The Bosnian Communist authorities, often jitterbugging to the tunes from Belgrade, confidentially briefed their members at closed Party meetings, one of which was attended by my mother, where, without naming anybody, they described what happened at the party, with many details made available by the good services of State Security. She nearly had a heart attack when she recalled my wearing the borrowed tall boots on the way to the party (the concept of which I had not bothered to explain to her), thus realizing that both of her children were there. She came back home shaken, and I offered a full confession, worrying all along that she might simply collapse. My mother's hair became all gray early and I am afraid much of it was due to my adventures.

In no time letters started pouring in to the Sarajevo press, coming from concerned citizens, some of whom were doubt-less part-time employees of State Security. Many unani-mously demanded that the names of the people involved in organizing a Nazi meeting in Sarajevo be released to the angry public, so that the cancerous outgrowth on the body of socialism could be dealt with immediately and merci-lessly. Due to pressure by the obedient public, the names of the "Nazi Nineteen" were happily announced in January 1987: there was a TV and radio-broadcast roll call, and the list was published in the papers the next day, for those who missed it the night before. Citizens started organizing spon-taneous meetings, which produced a slew of demands for severe punishment; university students had spontaneous meetings, some recalling the decadent performances at Club Volens-Nolens, concluding with whither-our-youth questions and demands for severe punishment as answers to those ques-tions; Liberation War veterans had spontaneous meetings, whereby they expressed their firm belief that work had no value in our families, and they also demanded severe punishment. My neighbors turned their heads away, passing me by; my fellow students boycotted an English-language class because I attended it, while the teacher quietly wept in the corner. Friends were banned by their parents from seeing us. The whole thing felt to me like reading a novel in which one of the characters—a feckless nihilistic prick—had my name. His life and my life intersected, indeed dramatically overlapped. At some point I started doubting the truth of my being. What if my reality was someone else's fiction? What if, I thought, I was the only one not seeing what the world was really like? What if I was the dead end of my own perception? What if I was just plain stupid?

Isidora, whose apartment was searched, all her papers taken by State Security, fled with her family to Belgrade and never came back. A few of us who stayed pooled our realities together. Goga had her appendix taken out, and was in the hospital, where nurses scoffed at her, and Guša, Veba, and I became closer than ever. We attended the spontaneous meetings, all in the vain hope that somehow our presence there would provide some sense of reality, that we could explain that it was all a bad performance/joke gone wrong, or that, in the end, it was nobody's business what we did at a private party. Various patriots and believers in socialist values at those meetings replayed the same good cop, bad cop games. At a Communist Party meeting I crashed at my college, as I had never been and would never be a Party member, a guy named Tihomir (the name could be translated as Quietpeace) was the bad cop. He kept yelling at me "You spat at my grandfather's bones!" and kept moaning in disbelief whenever I suggested that this was all just ridiculous, while the Party secretary, a nice young woman, kept unsuccessfully trying to placate him.

The Party, however, was now watching how we behaved. Or so I was told by a man who came to our home, sent by the County Committee of the Party, to check up on us. "Be careful," he said in an avuncular voice, "they are watching you very closely," whereupon I understood Kafka in a flash. (Only a few years later, the same man would come to our house to buy some honey from my father, who was dealing it out of our home. The man wouldn't talk about the events regarding the birthday party, except for saying "Such were the times." He would tell me that his ten-year-old daughter wanted to be a writer, and would show me a poem that she wrote, which he proudly carried in his wallet. The poem would look to me like a first draft of a suicide note, as the first line read: "I do not want to live, as nobody loves me." He would tell me that she was too shy to show him her poems—she would drop them, as if accidentally, so he could find them. I remember him walking away burdened with buckets of Hemon's honey. I hope his daughter is still alive.)

Eventually, the scandal noise fizzled out. On the one hand, a lot of people realized that the level of the hullaba-loo was inversely proportional to the true significance of the whole thing. We were scapegoated, as the Bosnian Commu-nists wanted to show that they would nip in the bud any attempt by young people to question the sacredness of socialist values. On the other hand, larger, far more serious scandals were to beset the hapless Communist regime. Within a few months, the government was unable to quell rumors about the collapse of the state company Agrokomerc, whose head was good friends with Central Committee big shots and created his mini-empire on nonexistent bonds, or the socialist version thereof. And there were people who were being arrested and publicly castigated for thinking and saying things that seriously questioned the undemocratic Communist rule and the pseudoreligious cult of Tito. Unlike ourselves, those people knew what they were talking about: they had developed ideas, they spoke from defined intellectual and political positions, their principles were a category different from confused late-adolescent feelings. Only later would I understand that we were our own stray dogs with flashlights, and then animal control arrived, and the only thing anyone would remember was the dog shit left behind.

For years afterward, I'd run into people who were still convinced that the birthday party was a fascist meeting, and they were as ready as ever to send us to the gallows. Understandably, I didn't always volunteer information about my involvement. Once, up in the wilderness of a mountain near Sarajevo, while called up in the army reserve, I shared the warmth of a campfire with drunken reservists who all thought that the birthday-party people should have been at least severely beaten. And I wholeheartedly agreed—indeed I claimed, perversely, that they should've been strung up, and got all excited about it. Such people, I said, should be tortured at length, and my distant-cousins-in-arms nodded in bloodthirsty agreement. I became someone else at that moment. I inhabited my enemy for a short time, and it felt both frightening and liberating. Let's drink to that, the reservists said, and we did.

The doubts about the reality of the whole thing kept

nagging at me for a long time. It didn't help matters that Isidora, now in Belgrade, did eventually become a downright, unabashed fascist. Belgrade in the nineties was fertile ground for the most virulent fascism, and she was at home there. She had public performances that celebrated the rich tradition of Serbian fascism. She dated a guy who would become a leader of a group of Serbian volunteers, cutthroats, and rapists known as the White Eagles, operating in Croatia and Bosnia at the time of the war. Later, she would write a memoir entitled *The Fiancée of a War Criminal*. Our friendship had long ceased, but I could not help questioning what had happened—maybe the fascist party had been concocted by her fascist part, obscure to me. Maybe I hadn't seen, blinded by the endless possibilities of Irrelevant Poetry, what she had seen; maybe I had been a pawn in her chess musical. Maybe my life had been like one of those Virgin Marys that show up in the frozen-food section of a supermarket in New Mexico or some such place—visible only to believers, ludicrous to everyone else.

3. THE LIFE AND WORK OF ALPHONSE KAUDERS

In 1987, in the wake of the birthday-party fiasco, I started working at a Sarajevo radio station, on a program geared toward younger urban people. It was called *Omladinski program* (The Youth Program), and everyone there was very young indeed, with very little or no radio experience. I failed the first, spring audition as the noise from the party still echoed in the radio studios, but was accepted in the fall, despite my mumbling, distinctly unradiophonic voice. The program was given some expression leeway by the radio heads, as the times were politically changing, but also because as young nobodies we could still take a fall if need be. I reported on cultural affairs, occasionally writing invectives against government idiocy and general stupidity, then reading them on the air. Soon I moved on to producing haughty film and book reviews in a voice of unquestionable (and unfounded) expertise.

All along, I was writing very short fiction. At some point I demanded and was given three or four minutes a week, which I used to air my stories on my friends Zoka and Neven's (now in Brno and London, respectively) pretty popular show. The time slot was called "Sasha Hemon Tells You True and Untrue Stories" (SHTYTUS). Some of the fiction embarrassed my family—already thoroughly embarrassed by the whole birthday-party debacle—because I had a series of stories about my cousin, a Ukrainian, in which he, for example, somehow lost all his limbs and lived a miserable life, until he got a job in a circus, where, night in, night out, elephants rolled him around the ring like a ball.

Around that time, I wrote the story "The Life and Work of Alphonse Kauders." It was evident to me that it would be hard to publish, as it made fun of Tito, contained a lot of lofty farts and low sex, and involved the characters of Hitler and Goebbels and such. Moreover, most of the literary magazines in Yugoslavia were at that time busily uncovering this or that national heritage, rediscovering writers whose poetry and prose could have easily fit in any anthology of irrelevant literature, but who would later be extremely busy warmongering. So I broke up the story into seven install-ments, each of which could fit into the three minutes of "SHTYTUS," and then wrote an introductory note for each of them—all insisting in the voice of unimpeachable exper-tise that I was a historian and that Alphonse Kauders was a historical figure and the subject of my extensive research. One of the introductory notes welcomed me upon my return from the archives of the USSR, where I had dug up revealing documents about Kauders. Another informed the listeners that I had just come back from Italy, where I was a guest at the convention of the Transnational Pornographic Party, whose platform was based on the teachings of the great Alphonse Kauders. Another one quoted letters from non-existent listeners who praised me for exhibiting the courage necessary for a historian, and proposed that I be appointed head of the radio station. Most of the time, I felt that nobody knew what I was doing, as nobody listened to "SHTYTUS," apart from my friends who generously gave me the airtime and the listeners who had no opportunity to change the sta-tion, as the whole thing was just too short. (One of the in-stallments was twenty-seven seconds long, shorter than the jingle for "SHTYTUS.") I didn't mind, as I wasn't all that eager to upset either the good cop or the bad cop.

After all seven installments were broadcast, I recorded the whole thing continuously, reading it with my mumble-voice (which is still fondly remembered by my friends as one of the worst to have ever graced the airwaves of Bosnia), providing some audio effects: Hitler's and Stalin's speeches, the chanting of obedient masses, Communist fighting songs, "Lili Marleen," the pernicious sound effects for the twentieth century. We broadcast the whole thing straight through, for twenty-some minutes with no breaks— a form of radio suicide—on Zoka and Neven's show, where-upon I was introduced as their guest in the studio, still pretending that I was a historian. I instructed my friends not to laugh under any circumstances (I'm afraid it's a very funny story). They read the listeners' letters, all of which were written by me, a few imitating the angry diction and spirit I had become familiar with after the infamous party. One letter demanded that I and people like me be strung up for de-filing sacred memories. Another demanded more respect for horses (as Alphonse Kauders hated horses), because horses taught us the values of hard work. Another objected to the representation of Gavrilo Princip, the assassin of the Austro-Hungarian archduke, and asserted that Princip *absolutely did not* pee his pants while waiting at a Sarajevo street cor-ner to shoot the heir to the imperial throne.

Then we opened the phone lines to the listeners. I'd thought (a) that nobody really listened to the Kauders series and (b) that those who did found it stupid and (c) that those who would believe it was true consisted of potheads, simpletons, and demented senior citizens, for whom the lines between history, fantasy, and radio programs were hopelessly blurred. Hence I was not prepared for questions or challenges nor was I intent on any further manipulation of false and dubious facts. The phones, however, were on fire, for an hour or so, live on air. The vast majority of people bought my Kauders story, and then offered many a tricky question or observation. A physician called and claimed that one cannot take out one's own appendix, as I claimed Kauders had done. A man called and said that he had in his hand the *Encyclopedia of Forestry*—where Kauders was supposed to have been featured extensively—and there was no trace of him in it. I came up with plausible answers, never laughing for a moment, inhabiting the historian character completely, fearing all the while that my cover might be blown, fretting—as I suspect actors do—at the possibility of the audience seeing the real, phony me behind the mask because my performance was completely transparent. I did manage to dismiss the fear of the good cop or the bad cop (probably the bad cop) calling in and ordering me to instantly come down to State Security headquarters again.

But the weirdest fear of all was that somebody might call in and say: "You liar! You know nothing about Kauders! I know far more than you do—and here is the true story!" Kauders became real at that moment—he was my Virgin appearing in the soundproof studio glass, behind which there was an indifferent sound engineer and a few people sparkling with the electricity of transgressive excitement. It was an exhilarating moment, when fantasy ruptured reality and overran it, much akin to the moment when the body rose from Dr. Frankenstein's surgical table and started choking him.

For months, even years, people would stop me and ask: "Did he really exist?" To some of them I said yes, to some of them I said no. But the fact of the matter is that there is no way of really knowing, as Kauders did exist for a flickering moment, like those subatomic particles in the nuclear accelerator in Switzerland, but not long enough for his existence to be physically recorded. The moment of his existence was too short for me to determine whether he was a mirage, a consequence of reaching the critical mass of collective delusion. Perhaps he had appeared to me just to let me understand that I'd been irreversibly irradiated by his malevolent aura.

I don't know where Herr Kauders might be now. Perhaps he is pulling the strings of fact and fiction, of untruth and truth, somehow making me write stories that I foolishly believe I imagine and invent. Perhaps one of these days I am going to get a letter signed A.K. (as he liked to sign his letters), telling me that the whole fucking charade is over, that the time of reckoning has come.

LIFE DURING WARTIME

■ ■ ■

In February 1991 I took an editorial position with the Sarajevo magazine *Naši dani* (Our Days), and instantly left my parents' home, where I was still embarrassingly lodging at the age of twenty-seven. With Davor and Pedja, two friends who also got jobs with the magazine, I rented a three-bedroom apartment in the old neighborhood Kovači. I had a full-time job and lived on my own—a major, adult accomplishment in a sadly socialist society where people grew old living with their parents, perpetually underemployed.

My previous and limited working experience had been in radio, where, apart from very short and baffling fiction, I wrote opinionated pieces on film, literature, and general stupidity. Hence I became the culture editor of *Naši dani*, and I somehow managed to negotiate thirteen pages for culture (whatever that was) out of the magazine's forty-eight. Convinced that the previous generation of journalists was tainted by the idiocy of comfortable communism, I refused to publish in my pages any writing by anyone older than twenty-seven, which required frequently fighting off the rest of the editorial team, still forgiving to some press veterans. I also wrote short, acerbic pieces for the satiric two-page spread and a column called "Sarajevo Republika," which I conceived of as "militantly urban." I was constantly high with being young and radical, reveling in the space of fuck-you-ness I carved out for myself.

The rest of the editorial team also came from radio, where we had shared contempt for the old socialist regime as well as for the politics of rabid nationalism, which was busy at the time dismantling the sorry remnants of Communist Yugoslavia. Our employer was the Liberal Party, which came out of what in the previous system was called the Association of Socialist Youth. (I wrote, for a fee, the culture part of the Liberal Party's platform.) We were hired, after the previous editorial team was fired in its entirety, for reasons I cannot really remember; I'd like to think that it was because our employer wanted a radical break—*Naši dani* had a forty-year history of publishing, largely marked by obedience to whatever was supposed to define socialist youth.

We had to learn quickly how to produce a biweekly magazine with a punch of immediacy. Alas, we soon had a chance: one of our first issues was largely devoted to (and supportive of) anti-Milošević demonstrations taking place in Belgrade, which he eventually crushed with the help of the Yugoslav People's Army's tanks. The blood of two young students was the first spilled by the army; we knew the flow would not stop there. By the spring, war was in full swing in Croatia. Reports of atrocities started coming in; we published photos of decapitated corpses and an interview with Vojislav Šešelj, a Serbian militia leader (now on trial in The Hague), who had famously promised to gouge Croatian eyes with rusty spoons. Somehow regular spoons were not bad enough.

At the onset of war, however, such things could still be treated as horrifying exceptions. One could indulge in thinking that a few bad apples had gone nuts, particularly since the Yugoslav/Serbian and Croatian authorities kept promising that everything would soon return to normal. But we soon broke a story on the army trucks transporting weapons (the cargo listed as "bananas") to the parts of Bosnia where Serbs constituted the majority. We covered the increasingly belligerent Bosnian parliament sessions and attended press conferences at which Radovan Karadžić (now on trial in The Hague), flanked by my former professor, pounded the table with his shovel-like fist, while making barely veiled threats of violence and war.

The more we knew about it, the less we wanted to know. The structure of our lives relied on the routine continuation of what we stubbornly perceived as normalcy. Hence, convinced that we were merely trying to live a normal life, we embarked upon a passionate pursuit of hedonistic oblivion. There was partying and drinking every night, often into the wee hours. We also danced a lot; indeed, I published an editorial in the cultural section, written by Guša, arguing that it was everybody's urgent duty to dance more if we wanted to stop the oncoming catastrophe.

Much of the money earned working for *Naši dani* I dropped into slot machines, so rigged as to preclude even a statistical probability of winning, because gambling results in a particularly intense oblivion. A more pleasurable means of denial was getting stoned and watching Vincente Minnelli's *Gigi*, often bellowing along: "Gigi, am I a fool without a mind / or have I really been too blind . . ." Pedja and I would occasionally get drunk in the afternoon and then croon along with Dean Martin, one of the great leaders of the international hedonist movement. We spent one splendid spring Saturday in our garden, eating spit-roasted lamb and smoking superb hashish (which, along with many other intoxicants, became widely available because the minister of the interior was controlling drug traffic). It made us ravenous, the hashish, so we ate lamb and smoked until we were so high we would've floated away, like balloons, toward the distant war-free landscapes, had we not been ballasted with enormous amounts of meat.

Those happy days before everything collapsed, when anything at all went far in inducing lifesaving oblivion! We did it all: staying up all night to close and lay out an issue of the magazine, subsisting on coffee and cigarettes and trance; consuming pornography and writing poetry; participating in passionate soccer-related discussions and endless, manic debates prompted by questions like: "Would you fuck a horse for a million deutschmarks?" or "Does the grandmaster Anatoly Karpov own a superfast speedboat?"

Then there was rampant, ecstatic promiscuity. A few ex-changed glances, sometimes in the presence of the boyfriend or girlfriend, were sufficient to arrange intercourse. The whole institution of dating seemed indefinitely suspended; it was no longer necessary to go out before hopping into bed. Indeed, there was no need for bed: building hallways, benches in parks, backseats of cars, bathtubs, and floors were just fine. We reveled in *Titanic* sex; there was no need for comfort or time for relationships on the sinking ship. It was a great fucking time, the short era of disaster euphoria, for nothing enhances pleasures and blocks guilt like a looming cataclysm. I'm afraid we are not taking advantage of the great opportunities pro-vided to us by this particular moment in human history.

By midsummer it became hard to maintain the precari-ous state of hysterical oblivion. A dealer we had used as a source for a story on drug traffic in Sarajevo went back home to Croatia for a visit and ended up forcibly conscripted, then called us, somehow, from the trenches, leaving a frenzied message: "You cannot imagine what is happening here!" We could hear shooting in the background. He didn't leave a number where we could reach him on the front line, and I doubt we would have called him back if he had. Then Pedja was dispatched to report from the Croatian front, only to be arrested and tortured by the Croatian forces. After his re-lease was negotiated, he returned all beaten up, appearing, aged, at our door. He couldn't sleep at night and moped around our place for days, his eyes glassy, his brain irrespon-sive to Dean Martin, his bruises changing color from deep blue to shallow yellow. Finally, annoyed, I sat him down, pushed a tape recorder into his face, and made him tell me about his experience in the Croatian war zone: his stupidly boarding a bus full of Croatian volunteers; the beating that ensued; the detention and the so-called interrogation; the humiliatingly stupid good cop, bad cop routine (the good cop liked the Pet Shop Boys); the squeezed testicles and kidney punching; the taste of the gun in his mouth; et cetera. When he finished, I turned off the recorder, ritually handed over to him the ninety-minute tape, and said: "Now put it away and let's move on." I deemed myself wise back then.

But there was nowhere to go. In July, I quit the editing job and went for a few weeks to Ukraine, just in time for the August putsch, the collapse of the USSR, and the subsequent Ukrainian independence. When I came back to Sarajevo in early September, the magazine had been shut down; Pedja and Davor had moved us all out of the Kovači apartment and back to our respective parents' homes, as we had no more money to pay the rent. The city was deflated, the euphoria exhausted. One night, I went to the Olympic Museum café, where we used to hang out a lot, and I watched glassy-eyed people stare into the terrible distance, barely talking to one another, some of them drugged to the brim, some of them naturally paralyzed, all of them terrified with what was now undeniable: it was all over. The war had arrived and now we were all waiting to see who would live, who would kill, and who would die.

THE MAGIC MOUNTAIN

■ ■ ■

My family used to have a cabin on the mountain called Jahorina, twenty miles from Sarajevo. Jahorina was a ski resort, and back in our teenagehood, Kristina and I spent our entire monthlong winter breaks skiing and partying, our parents coming up only on weekends to deliver food and clean clothes and assess the damage. While in the winter the mountain was full of skiers, tourists, and friends, it was mostly depopulated in the summer. On weekends, there would be a few other cabin owners who, like my parents, escaped from the city heat to tinker with woodwork. Kristina and I avoided going to the mountain in the summer, despite our parents' insistence that Jahorina was heaven, as compared with the hell of Sarajevo. We much preferred idling and simmering in the parentless cauldron of the city.

But sometime in the late eighties, I started going up to the mountain in the summer. I'd pack my little Fićo (the Yugoslav replica of the Fiat 500) with books and music and move to Jahorina for a month at a time. I was in my mid-twenties, still living with my parents, which, apart from problems pertinent to my personal sovereignty and privacy, made reading with sustained attention fairly difficult—my parents constantly demanded participation in family activities and devised elaborate chores. In the Jahorina cabin, on the other hand, I could be fully in charge of my own time, which I regimented like a monk, reading eight to ten hours a day. I'd step out of my monastic devotion only to attend to the needs of my foolish body, which besides food and coffee, demanded some physical exertion. Hence I chopped firewood and occasionally went for long hikes farther up the mountain, above the tree line, toward harsh, barren landscapes and peaks from which the poignant expanse of Bosnia could be seen. I eschewed other people and went on foot to the solitary supermarket, a couple of miles away, only when I needed more cigarettes or wine.

For weeks before my move to the mountain, I'd be assembling my reading list: from le Carré's Smiley novels (which for years I reread every summer) to scholarly works on the origins of the Old Testament myths; from anthologies of contemporary American short stories to the Corto Maltese comic books. There was always a particular benefit from reading for ten hours straight: I'd enter a kind of hypersensitive exaltation that allowed me to average four hundred pages a day. The book would become a vast, intricate space in my head, and I couldn't leave it, not when I ate, not when I hiked, not when I slept—I lived inside it. During the week it took to read *War and Peace*, Bolkonsky and Natasha showed up in my dreams regularly.

I was prone to anxiety and depression in my twenties, which I experienced as depletion of my interiority, as a drought of thought and language. The purpose of going to the mountain was to replenish my mind, to reboot the language apparatus, the thought machine. But my reclusion worried my parents, while my friends suspected I was in the process of losing my mind. At night, the only sounds were the lows and bells of roaming cattle, the wind and the branches scratching the roof. Excited birds would bid me good early morning, and I'd start reading as soon as I opened my eyes. I enjoyed my life ascetically simplified: reading, eating, hiking, sleeping. The self-imposed austerity remedied whatever pain I'd carried up to the mountain.

The last time I went to Jahorina to read was in late September 1991. Much of the summer of 1991, I'd spent in Ukraine, witnessing the demise of the Soviet Union and Ukraine's independence. Over the summer, the war in Croatia had rapidly progressed from incidents to massacres, from skirmishes to the Yugoslav People's Army's completely destroying the town of Vukovar. When I returned to Sarajevo at the end of August, the war had already settled in people's minds: fear, confusion, and drugs reigned. I had no money, so Pedja offered me hack work in a porn magazine he was planning to start, convinced that people would lap it up as distraction from the oncoming disaster. I declined, because I didn't want bad sex writing (as though there were any other kind) to be the last thing I'd done if I were to be killed in the war. I packed a carful of books and moved up to the cabin to read and write as much as possible before the war consigned everything and all to death and oblivion.

I stayed in Jahorina through December. My monastic mountain living was now about rudimentary thought protection, for once war got inside my mind, I feared, it would burn and pillage it. I read *The Magic Mountain* and Kafka's letters; I wrote stuff full of madness, death, and whimsical wordplay; I listened to Miles Davis, who died that fall, while staring at the embers in our fireplace. On my hikes I conducted imaginary conversations with imaginary partners, not unlike the ones between Castorp and Settembrini in Mann's novel. I chopped a lot of wood to ease my rising anxiety. Occasionally, I climbed a steep mountain face without any gear or protection. It was a kind of suicidal self-soothing challenge: if I made it all the way to the top without falling, I thought, I could survive the war. One of the daily rituals was watching the nightly news broadcast at 7:30, and the news was never good, always worse.

Years later, in Chicago, I'd struggle to perform exercises that were supposed to help me with managing my anger: upon the advice of my ever-grinning therapist, I'd try to control my breathing while envisioning in detail a place I associated with peace and safety. I'd invariably invoke our cabin in Jahorina and spend long stretches of time recalling the smallest details: the smooth surface of the wooden table my father built without using a single nail; a cluster of old ski passes hanging under the mute cuckoo clock; the indestructible fridge my parents moved to the mountain from our Sarajevo home, whose brand name—Obod Cetinje—was the first thing I read by myself. In the therapy sessions, I remembered how solitary reading cleared my cluttered mind, how the hurt was somehow healed by the ubiquitous smell of pine, by the high-altitude air crispness, by the morning angle of mountain light.

Toward the end of my stay in the fall of '91, our Irish setter, Mek, kept me company. Still a puppy, he would be up with the birds in the morning and lick my cheeks and forehead, covering them with a thick coating of saliva. I'd let him out to do whatever puppies do at the crack of dawn, while I went back to bed to read, or continue a dream rife with literary characters. One morning, after I'd let him out, the sounds of shooting startled me while I was immersed in a book. When I looked outside, I saw a military police unit, identifiable by their white belts. They were shooting blanks at imaginary enemies, wearing gas masks, charging uphill past the cabin. In their midst was Mek, who in his puppy idiocy was running, prancing, and barking at them. A blank from close range could obviously kill him, so, book in hand,

I ran after the charging MP unit in my pajamas, hopelessly summoning Mek to heel. He didn't heed my calls and I caught up only when the unit stopped for a breather. They took off their gas masks and panted, sweat pouring down their faces, while I incoherently apologized for some perceived fault of mine. They said nothing, too exhausted and invested in their war rehearsal. As I stumbled downhill in my slippers, dragging Mek by the collar, they assumed new combat positions. For all I knew they might have pointed their guns at me.

Another morning, in early December, I sat despondent and cold, drinking tepid tea, too tired to start a fire. Mek placed his head in my lap for petting. I gazed into the bleak fog outside and wondered what would happen to all of us. My mind was so defeated by the unstoppable advance of war that there was no longer a book to read or a story to write that could possibly help it ever recover. At the very moment I reached the deepest recess of despair, the phone rang—or at least that is how my memory has edited that particular scene—and a woman from the American Cultural Center told me that I had been invited to visit the United States for a month under the auspices of the United States Information Agency. I'd had an interview with the head of the Cultural Center earlier that summer, but had expected nothing from it and pretty much forgot all about it. Indeed, I thought for a long moment that it was a prank call of some sort, but when she told me I needed to stop by the center to work out the details of my visit, I promised her I would. I hung up the phone and started building the fire. The following day, I left the mountain.

LET THERE BE WHAT CANNOT BE
■ ■ ■

On October 14, 1991, Radovan Karadžić spoke at a session of the Bosnian and Herzegovinian Parliament, which had been debating a referendum on independence from the Yugoslavia crippled by the secession of Slovenia and Croatia earlier that year. Karadžić was there to warn the parliament against following the Slovenes and Croats down "the highway of hell and suffering."

I was in Jahorina at that time, placating myself with reading and writing. I turned on the nightly news to watch him thunder at the frazzled members of the parliament: "Do not think you will not lead Bosnia and Herzegovina into hell and the Muslim people into possible annihilation, as the Muslim people cannot defend themselves in case of war here." Throughout his tirade, in a manner familiar to me from the press conferences I had attended, he clutched the lectern edges, as though about to hurl it at his feeble audience. But then he let go of it to stab the air with his forefinger at the word *annihilation*. The Bosnian president, Alija Izetbegović, a Muslim, was visibly distressed.

You can easily find a grainy YouTube clip of Karadžić's ranting. The Internet and television can convert just about anything into benign banality, but his performance is still bloodcurdling. Karadžić was then president of the hard-line nationalist Serbian Democratic Party, which had already acquired control of the parts of Bosnia with a Serbian majority, but he was not a member of the parliament, nor did he hold any elective office. He was there simply because he could. His very presence rendered the parliament weak and unimportant; backed by the Serb-dominated Yugoslav People's Army, he spoke from the position of unimpeachable power over the life and death of the people the parliament represented. And he knew it and liked it.

Tranquilized by the weeks of therapeutic reading (Kafka, Mann), I could not initially comprehend what Karadžić meant by "annihilation." I groped for a milder, less terrifying interpretation—perhaps he meant "historical irrelevance"? I could settle for historical irrelevance, whatever it meant. What he was saying was well outside the scope of my humanist imagination, prone to reveries and fears; his words extended far beyond the habits of normalcy I desperately clung to as war loomed over what Sarajevans called "common life."

The parliament eventually decided a referendum was the way to go. It took place in February 1992; the Serbs boycotted it while the majority of Bosnians voted for independence. Throughout March, there were barricades on the streets of Sarajevo, much shooting in the mountains around it. In April, Karadžić's snipers aimed at a peaceful antiwar demonstration in front of the parliament building, and two women were killed. On May 2, Sarajevo was cut off from the rest of the world and the longest siege in modern history began. By the end of the summer, nearly every front page in the universe had published a picture from a Serbian death camp. By that time, I understood that Karadžić had wagged the stick of genocide at the Bosnian Muslims in his address to the hapless Bosnian Parliament, while the unappetizing carrot was their bare survival. "Don't make me do it," he was essentially saying. "For I will be perfectly at home in the hell I create for you."

Now I have little doubt that, regardless of the outcome of the parliamentary session, Karadžić would have gladly sped in his motorcade down the hell-and-suffering highway. What I didn't see then is clear to me now: the possibility of war not happening was already completely foreclosed. The annihilation machine was happily revving, everything was in place for the genocide operations, the purpose of which was not only the destruction and displacement of Bosnian Muslims but also the unification of the ethnically pure lands into a Greater Serbia. Why had he staged that performance before the parliament, since peace was never an option? Why did he bother?

I have spent time trying to comprehend how everything I

had known and loved came violently apart; I have been busy obsessively parsing the details of the catastrophe to understand how it could have taken place. After Karadžić's arrest, I watched the YouTube clip, trying to figure out why he had bothered. Now I know: the point of that performance was the performance itself. It was not meant for the beleaguered Bosnian Parliament but for the patriotic Serbs watching the broadcast, for those ready to embark upon an epic project that would take sacrifice, murder, and ethnic cleansing to be completed. Karadžić was showing his people that he was as tough and determined a leader as need be, yet neither unwise nor unreasonable. He was indicating that war would not be a rash decision on his part, while capable of recognizing that genocide might be inescapable. If there was a difficult job to be done, he was going to do it unflinchingly and ruthlessly. He was the leader who was going to lead his people through the hell of murder to the land where honor and salvation awaited them.

The model for Karadžić's role was provided by Petar Petrović Njegoš's epic poem *The Mountain Wreath* (*Gorski vijenac*). Just like everyone else, I was forced to study it in school as it was part of the socialist cannon, easy to interpret within the framework of "freedom," widely available in Tito's Yugoslavia. Set at the end of the seventeenth century and published in 1847, it is deeply embedded in the tradition of Serbian epic poetry; a foundational text of Serbian cultural nationalism, it always bored me to tears. Its central character is Vladika Danilo, the bishop and sovereign of

Montenegro, the only Serbian territory unconquered at the time by the powerful and all-encroaching Ottoman Empire. Vladika Danilo thinks he has a major problem: some Montenegrin Serbs have converted to Islam. For him, they are the fifth column of the Turks, a people who could never be trusted, a permanent threat to the freedom and sovereignty of the Serbian people.

Wise leader that he is, Vladika Danilo summons a council to help him find the solution. He listens to the advice of various bloodthirsty warriors: "Without suffering no song is sung," one of them says, decasyllabically. "Without suffering no saber is forged." He receives a delegation of Muslims pleading for peace and coexistence and all that; they are offered a chance to keep their heads on their shoulders by converting back to "the faith of their forefathers." He speaks of freedom and the difficult decisions required to protect it: "The wolf is entitled to a sheep / Much like a tyrant to a feeble man. / But to stomp the neck of tyranny / To lead it to the righteous knowledge / That is man's most sacred duty."

In lines familiar to nearly every Serbian child and adult, Vladika Danilo eventually recognizes that the total, ruthless extermination of the Muslims is the only way: "Let there be endless struggle," he says. "Let there be what cannot be." He will lead his people through the hell of murder and onward to honor and salvation: "On the grave flowers will grow / For a distant future generation."

Karadžić, who grew up in the part of Bosnia where mail

is delivered by wolves (as we used to say in Sarajevo), was intimately familiar with Serbian epic poetry. A skillful player of the gusle, a single-string fiddle (for which no real skill is required) used to accompany the oral performance of epic poems, he understood his role in the blazing light cast by Vladika Danilo. He recognized himself in the martyrdom of leadership; he believed that he was the one to finish the job that Vladika Danilo started. He was to be the hero in an epic poem that would be sung by a distant future generation.

Indeed, while hiding in plain sight in Belgrade, under-cover as a New Age mountebank, Karadžić frequented a bar called Mad House—*Luda kuća*. Mad House offered weekly gusle-accompanied performances of Serbian epic poetry; wartime pictures of him and General Ratko Mladić, the Bosnian Serbs' military leader (now on trial in The Hague), proudly hung on the walls. A local newspaper claimed that, on at least one occasion, Karadžić performed an epic poem in which he himself featured as the main hero, undertaking feats of extermination. Consider the horrible postmodern-ism of the situation: an undercover war criminal narrating his own crimes in decasyllabic verse, erasing his personality so that he could assert it more forcefully and heroically.

The tragic, heartbreaking irony of it all is that Karadžić played out his historical, pseudoheroic role in less than ten years. In the flash of his infernal pan hundreds of thousands died, millions (including my family) were displaced, untold numbers of people paid in pain for his induction into the pantheon of Serbian epic poetry. After his arrest in the grotesque guise of a spiritual quack, one can imagine him singing of himself as a wise sage for his prison mates in The Hague.

If you're a writer, it is hard not to see a kind of Shakespeare-for-Idiots lesson in the story of Radovan Karadžić: his true and only home was the hell he created for others. Before he became the leader of the Bosnian Serbs and after he was forced out by the Serbian president Slobodan Milošević (who was Karadžić's supporter until he exhausted his usefulness), Karadžić was a prosaic nobody. A mediocre psychiatrist, a minor poet, and a petty embezzler before the war, at the time of his arrest he was a full-fledged charlatan with a clump of hair tied on his forehead to attract cosmic energy. It was only during the war, performing on a blood-soaked stage, that he could fully develop his inhuman potential. He was what he was because what could not happen did in the end happen.

DOG LIVES

■ ■ ■

When I was a kid, I brought home many a mangy puppy I'd found on the streets. I'd arrange sofa cushions into a soft bed, then go to school and leave my would-be pet to enjoy its new life, hoping that, when the puppy felt sufficiently at home, it'd be ready to commit to a lifelong friendship with me. But when my parents returned home from work, they'd find our house an unreal mess: the puppy had chewed up the cushions and peed on the floor. Quickly would my lifelong-friend candidate be evicted onto the brutal streets of Sarajevo.

Both of my parents were born into poor peasant households, dependent on the toil of farm animals, where the notion of having a pet could not exist. Hence I'd find myself passionately arguing with Mother and Father for my right to own a dog. My family was not a democratic institution and I was sternly made to understand that my obligations to the family exceeded all other duties and passions. As for rights, there was no family charter guaranteeing anything to me other than food, shelter, education, and love. The final, rusty nail in the coffin for my pet-owning hopes was my mother's hard-to-counter argument that, since I never really cleaned up after myself, I most certainly would not clean up after a dog.

But my sister, Kristina, was (and still is) a strong-headed force of nature. While I often found myself fighting for my right to discuss my right to have rights, my determined sister had a different and a much more efficient approach. She wasted no time debating her rights with our parents; she simply acted as though she axiomatically possessed them and exercised them as she saw fit.

She first brought in a Siamese cat, which died from a form of peritonitis so rare that we donated his little corpse to a researcher at a vet school. The next cat was a piebald country girl, which we let out of the apartment onto the street, until she was run over by a car. Our heartbroken mother absolutely forbade any new pets entering our home; she could not, she said, handle the loss.

Kristina, having long asserted her unimpeachable right to do whatever she felt like, completely ignored the prohibition. In the spring of 1991, she recruited her new boyfriend to drive with her to Novi Sad, a town in northern Serbia a couple of hundred miles away from Sarajevo, where she'd somehow tracked down a breeder. With the money she'd saved from her modeling gigs, she bought a gorgeous, blazingly auburn Irish setter puppy and brought him home. Father was shocked—dogs in the city were self-evidently useless, a resplendent Irish setter even more so—and unconvincingly demanded that she return him to the breeder immediately; naturally, she ignored him. Mother offered some predictable rhetorical resistance to yet another creature she'd worry about excessively, but it was clear she had fallen in love with the dog on the spot. Within a day or two he chewed up someone's shoe and was instantly forgiven. We named him Mek.

—

In a small city like Sarajevo no one can live in isolation, and all experiences end up shared. Around the time of Mek's arrival, my best friend, Veba, who lived across the street from us, acquired a dog himself, a German shepherd named Don. Čika-Vlado, Veba's father, a low-ranking officer of the Yugoslav People's Army, was working at a military warehouse near Sarajevo where a guard dog gave birth to a litter of puppies. Veba picked the slowest, clumsiest puppy, as he knew that, if they were to be destroyed, that one would be the first to go.

Veba had been Kristina's first boyfriend and the only one I'd ever really liked. They started going out in high school and broke up a couple of years later; my sister was initially upset, but he and I stayed close. We were often inseparable, particularly after we'd started playing in a band together. Once my sister got over their breakup, they renewed their friendship. Soon after the puppies arrived, they'd often take them out for a walk at the same time. No longer living with my parents, I often came home for food and family time, particularly after Mek had come—I loved to take him out, my childhood dream of owning a pet fulfilled by my indomitable sister. Veba and I would walk with Mek and Don by the river, or sit on a bench and watch them roll in the grass while we smoked and talked about music and books, girls and movies, our dogs gnawing playfully at each other's throats. I don't know how dogs really become friends, but Mek and Don were as close friends as Veba and I were.

The last time I remember the dogs being together was when we went up to Jahorina to mark the arrival of 1992. Apart from my sister and me and our friends—ten humans in total—there were also three dogs: in addition to Mek and Don, our friend Guša brought along Laki, an energetic dog of indeterminate breed (Guša called him a cocktail spaniel). In the restricted space of the smallish mountain cabin, the humans would trip over the dogs, while they'd often get into their canine arguments and would have to be pulled apart. One night, playing a card game called Preference into the wee hours, Guša and I got into a screaming argument, which made the dogs crazy—there was enough barking and screaming to blow the roof off. I recall that moment with warmth, for all the intense intimacy of our shared previous life was in it. I didn't know then that the week we spent together would amount to a farewell party to our common Sarajevo life. A couple of weeks later, I departed for the United States, never to return to our mountain cabin.

My sister and Veba still remember the last time Mek and Don were together: it was April 1992; they took them for a walk in a nearby park; there was shooting up in the hills around Sarajevo; a Yugoslav People's Army plane menacingly broke the sound barrier above the city; the dogs barked like crazy. They said: "See you later!" to each other as they parted, but would not see each other for five years.

Soon thereafter, my sister followed her latest boyfriend to Belgrade. My parents stayed behind for a couple of weeks, during which sporadic gunfire and shelling increased daily. More and more often, they spent time with their neighbors in the improvised basement shelter, trying to calm Mek down. On May 2, 1992, with Mek in tow, they took a train out of Sarajevo before all the exits were closed and the relentless siege commenced. Soon the station was subjected to a rocket attack; no train would leave the city for ten years or so.

My parents were heading to the village in northwestern Bosnia where my father was born, a few miles from the town of Prnjavor, which came under Serb control. My dead grandparents' house still stood on a hill called Vučijak (translatable as Wolfhill). Father had been keeping beehives on the family homestead and insisted on leaving Sarajevo largely because it was time to prepare the bees for the summer. In willful denial of a distinct possibility that they might not return for a long time, they brought no warm clothes or passports, just a small bag of summer clothes.

They spent the first few months of the war on Vučijak, their chief means of sustenance my father's beekeeping and my mother's vegetable garden. Convoys of drunken Serbian soldiers passed by on their way to an ethnic-cleansing operation or from the front line, singing songs of slaughter and angrily shooting in the air. My parents, cowering in the house, secretly listened to news from the besieged Sarajevo. Mek sometimes happily chased after the military trucks and my parents desperately ran after him, calling him, terrified that the drunken soldiers might shoot him for malicious fun. When there were no trucks and soldiers around, Mek would run up and down the slopes, remembering, perhaps—or so I'd like to imagine—our days in Jahorina.

Sometime that summer, Mek fell ill. He could not get to his feet; he refused food and water, there was blood in his urine. My parents laid him on the floor in the bathroom, which was the coolest space in the house. Mother stroked him and talked to him while he kept looking straight into her eyes—she always claimed he understood everything she told him. They called the vet, but the vet's office had only one car at its disposal, which was continuously on the road, attending to all the sick animals in the area. It took the vet a couple of days to finally arrive. He instantly recognized that Mek was infested with deer ticks, all of them bloated with his blood, poisoning him. The prognosis was not good, he said, but at the office he could give him a shot that might help. My father borrowed my uncle's tractor and cart in which pigs were normally transported to slaughter. He put the limp Mek in the cart and drove down the hill, all the way to Prnjavor, to get the shot that could save his life. On his way, the Serb Army trucks passed him, the soldiers looking down on the panting Mek.

The magic shot worked and Mek lived, recovering after a few days. But then it was my mother's turn to get terribly sick. Her gall bladder was full of stones and infected—back in Sarajevo, she'd been recommended a surgery to remove them, which she'd feared and kept postponing, and then the war broke out. Her brother, my uncle Milisav, drove down from Subotica, a town at the Serbian-Hungarian border, and took her back with him for urgent surgery. Father had to wait for his friend Dragan to come and get Mek and him. While Father was preparing his beehives for his long absence, Mek would lie nearby, stretched in the grass, keeping him company.

Dragan arrived a couple of days later. On the way in, he was stopped at the checkpoint at the top of Vučijak. The men were hairy, drunk, and impatient. They asked Dragan where he was going, and when he explained that my father was waiting for him, they menacingly told him they'd been watching my father closely for a while, that they knew all about his family (which was ethnically Ukrainian—earlier that year the Ukrainian church in Prnjavor had been blown up by the Serbs), and they were well aware of his son (of me, that is), who had written against the Serbs and was now in America. They were just about ready to take care of my father once and for all, they told Dragan. The men belonged to a paramilitary unit that called itself Vukovi (the Wolves) and were led by one Veljko, whom a few years earlier my father had thrown out of a meeting he'd organized to discuss bringing in running water from a nearby mountain well. Veljko would later go to Austria to pursue a rewarding criminal career, only to return right before the war to put his paramilitary unit together. "You let Hemon know we're coming," the Wolves told Dragan as they let him through.

When Dragan reported the incident, which he took very seriously, my father thought it would be better to try to get out as soon as possible than wait for them to come at night and slit his throat. At the checkpoint, the guard shift had just changed and the new men were not drunk or churlish enough to care, so my father and Dragan were waved through. The checkpoint Wolves failed to sniff out or see Mek, because Father kept him down on the floor. Later on, in their mindless rage, or, possibly, trying to steal the honey, the Wolves destroyed my father's hives. (In a letter he'd send to Chicago he'd tell me that of all the losses the war inflicted upon him, losing his bees was the most painful.)

On their way toward the Serbian border, Father and Dragan passed many checkpoints. Father was concerned that if those manning the checkpoints saw a beautiful Irish setter, they'd immediately understand that he was coming from a city, as there were few auburn Irish setters in the Bosnian countryside, largely populated by mangy mutts and wolves. Moreover, the armed men could easily get pissed at someone trying to save a fancy dog in the middle of a war, when people were being killed left and right. At each checkpoint, Mek would try to get up and my father would press him down with his hand, whispering calming words into his ear; Mek would lie back down. He never produced a sound, never insisted on standing up, and, miraculously, no one at the checkpoints noticed him. My father and Dragan made it out, across the border and on to Subotica.

Meanwhile, in Sarajevo under siege, Veba was conscripted into the Bosnian Army, defending the city from the former Yugoslav People's Army, now transformed overnight into the genocidal Serb Army. Veba's father, on the other hand, was on duty at his warehouse outside Sarajevo when the hostilities flared up and was arrested by the Bosnians soon after the fighting began. Veba and his family would have no news from him for a couple of years, not knowing whether he was alive or dead.

While my family was scattered all over elsewhere, Veba's still lived across the street from our home. He was sharing a small apartment with his girlfriend, mother, brother, and Don. Very quickly, food became scarce—a good dinner under siege was a slice of bread sprinkled with oil; rice was all that was available for most of the people, meal after meal, day after day. Packs of abandoned dogs roamed the city, sometimes attacking humans or tearing up fresh corpses. To have and feed a dog was a suspicious luxury, yet Veba's family shared with Don whatever they had—all of them were now skin and bones. Frequently, there was nothing to share and Don somehow understood the difficulty of the situation and never begged. During shelling, Don would pace around their apartment, sniffing and squealing. He'd calm down only when all of Veba's family were in the same room; he'd lie down and watch them all closely. Every once in a while, they'd entertain him by asking: "Where is Mek? Where is Mek?" and Don would run to the front door and bark excitedly, remembering his friend.

When they took Don out to pee, Veba and his family had to stay within a narrow space protected by their high-rise from the Serb snipers. The children played with him and he let them pet him. Within weeks, Don developed an uncanny ability to sense an imminent mortar-shell attack: he'd bark and move anxiously in circles; bristling, he'd jump on Veba's mother's shoulders and push her until she and everyone else rushed back into the building. A moment later, shells would start exploding nearby.

My father and Mek eventually joined my mother in Subotica. When she had sufficiently recovered from her gall-bladder surgery, my parents moved to Novi Sad, not far away, where Mother's other brother owned a little one-bedroom apartment in which they could stay. They spent a year or so there, trying all along to get the necessary papers to emigrate to Canada. During that time, Father was often gone for weeks, working in Hungary with Dragan's construction company. Mek's constant presence and my sister's occasional visits provided Mother with her only comfort. She longed for Sarajevo, horrified by what was happening in Bosnia, insulted by the relentless Serbian propaganda pouring out of the TV and radio. She spent days crying, and Mek would put his head in her lap and look up at her with his moist setter eyes, and Mother confided in him as her only friend. Every day, she had a hard time confronting the fact that they'd lost everything they'd worked for their whole lives; the only remnant of their previous life was the gorgeous Irish setter.

The one-bedroom in Novi Sad was often full of refugees from Bosnia—friends of friends or family of family—whom my parents put up until the unfortunate people could make it to Germany or France or some other place where they were not wanted and never would be. They slept scattered all over the floor, my mother stepping over the bodies on her way to the bathroom, Mek always at her heels. He never bothered the refugees, never barked at them. He let the children pet him.

Young male that he was, Mek would often brawl with other dogs. Once, when my mother took him out, he got into a confrontation with a mean Rottweiler. She tried to separate them, unwisely, as they were about to go at each other's throats, and the Rottweiler tore my mother's hand apart. Kristina was there at the time, and she took Mother to the emergency room, where they had absolutely nothing to treat the injury; they did give her the address of a doctor who could sell them bandages and a tetanus shot. They didn't have enough to pay the fare back home, and the cabdriver said he'd come the next day to get the rest of the money. My sister bluntly told him that there was no reason for him to come back, for they'd have no money tomorrow, or the day after tomorrow, or anytime soon. (The cabbie didn't insist: the daily inflation in Serbia at that time was about 300 percent, and the money would have been worthless by the next day anyway.) For years afterward, Mother could not move her hand properly or grip anything with it. Mek would go crazy if he but sniffed a Rottweiler on the same block.

In the fall of 1993, my parents and sister finally got all the papers and the plane tickets for Canada. Family and friends came over to bid them farewell. Everyone was sure they'd never see them again. There were a lot of tears, as at a funeral. Mek figured out that something was up; he never let my mother or father out of his sight, as if worried they might leave him; he became especially cuddly, putting his head into their laps whenever he could, leaning against their shins when lying down. Touched though my father may have been with Mek's love, he didn't want to take him along to Canada—he couldn't know what was waiting for them there; where they'd live, whether they'd be able to take care of themselves, let alone a dog. My mother could not bring herself to discuss the possibility of moving to Canada without Mek; she just wept at the very thought of leaving him with strangers.

Back in Sarajevo, Veba got married, and he and his wife moved out of the place across the street from us. Don stayed with Veba's mother and brother because Veba's duties kept him away from home for long stretches, while his wife, working for the Red Cross, was also often gone. Following a Red Cross official on an inspection of a Bosnian POW camp, Veba's wife discovered that his father was alive. Ever since he'd failed to return home from work at the beginning of the war, Don— prompted by the question "Where is Vlado?"—would leap at the coatrack where Veba's father used to hang up his uniform. Although čika-Vlado would be released from the POW camp toward the end of the war, Don would never see him again.

I received only intermittent news from Veba's family— Veba's letters mailed by a foreign friend who could go in and out of the Bosnian war zone; a sudden, late-night call from a satellite phone, arranged by a friend who worked for a foreign-journalist pool. During the siege the regular phone lines were most often down, but every once in a while they would inexplicably work, so I'd randomly try to reach my best friend. One late night in 1994, I called Veba's family from Chicago on a whim. It was very early morning in Sarajevo, but Veba's mother picked up the phone after one ring. She was sobbing uncontrollably, so my first thought was that Veba had been killed. She composed herself enough to tell me that my friend was fine, but that someone had poisoned their dog. Don had been in horrible pain all night, retching and vomiting yellow slime, she said; he'd died just a short while before I called. Veba was there too; upon hearing the news, he'd biked from his new place in the middle of the night, the curfew still on, risking his life. He'd made it in time to hold Don as he expired, and was crying on the phone with me. I could find no words for him, as I could never provide any consolation for my friends under siege. Veba wrapped Don in a blanket, carried him down the fifteen flights of stairs, and buried him with his favorite tennis ball behind the high-rise.

My father recognized how inconsolable my mother would be without Mek and finally surrendered. In December 1993, my parents, my sister, and Mek arrived in Canada, and I rushed over from Chicago to see them. As soon as I walked in the door of their barely furnished fifteenth-floor apartment in Hamilton, Ontario, Mek ran toward me, wagging his tail, happy to see me. I was astonished he remembered me after nearly three years. I'd felt that large parts of my Sarajevo self had vanished, but when Mek put his head in my lap, some of me came back.

Mek had a happy life in Hamilton. My mother always said that he was a "lucky boy." He died in 2007, at the age of seventeen. My parents would never consider having a dog again. My mother confides in a parakeet these days, and cries whenever Mek is mentioned.

Veba moved to Canada in 1998. He lives in Montreal with his wife and children. After years of Veba's refusing to consider having another dog, a lovely husky mix named Kahlua is now part of his family. My sister lives in London; she has not had a dog since Mek. I married a woman who has never lived without a dog, and we now have a Rhodesian ridgeback named Billie.

THE BOOK OF MY LIFE

■ ■ ■

Professor Nikola Koljević had the long, slender fingers of a piano player. Although he was now a literature professor—he was my teacher at the University of Sarajevo in the late eighties—as a student he'd supported himself by playing the piano in the jazz bars of Belgrade. He'd even had gigs as a member of a circus orchestra—he'd sit at the fringe of the arena, I imagined, with a Shakespeare tragedy open above the piano keys, flexing his fingers, ignoring the lions, waiting for the clowns to enter.

Professor Koljević taught a course in poetry and criticism, for which we read poetry with a critical slant—the New Critic Cleanth Brooks was his patron saint. In his class we learned how to analyze the inherent properties of a piece of literature, disregarding politics, biography, or anything external to the text. Most of the other teachers delivered their lectures passionlessly, even haughtily; possessed by the demons of scholastic boredom, they asked for nothing in particular from us. In Professor Koljević's class, on the other hand, we unpacked poems like Christmas presents and the solidarity of common discoveries filled the small, hot room on the top floor of the Faculty of Philosophy.

He was incredibly well read. He often quoted Shakespeare in English off the top of his head, which always impressed me; I, too, wanted to have read everything and to be able to quote with ease. He also taught an essay-writing course—the only writing course I've ever taken—where we read the classic essayists, beginning with Montaigne, and then tried to produce some lofty-seeming thoughts, coming up with hapless imitations instead. Still, it was flattering that he found it even remotely possible we could write something belonging to the same universe as Montaigne. It made us feel as if we had been personally invited to participate in the fine, gentle business of literature.

Once, Professor Koljević told us about the book his daughter had begun writing at the age of five. She had titled it "The Book of My Life," but had written only the first chapter. She planned to wait for more life to accumulate, he told us, before starting Chapter 2. We laughed, still in our early chapters, oblivious to the malignant plots accelerating all around us.

After I'd graduated, I phoned to thank Professor Koljević for what he'd taught me, for introducing me to the world that could be conquered by reading. Back then, calling him was a brave act for a student ever in awe of his professors, but he was not put out. He invited me for an evening stroll by the Miljacka River, and we discussed literature and life as friends and equals. He put his hand on my shoulder as we walked, his fingers cramped like hooks as he held on, for I was considerably taller than he. It was uncomfortable, but I said nothing. He had, flatteringly, crossed a border, and I did not want to undo the closeness.

Not long after our stroll, I began working as an editor for *Naši dani*. At around the same time, Professor Koljević became one of the highest-positioned members of the Serbian Democratic Party (SDS), a virulently nationalist organization, headed by Karadžić, the talentless poet destined to become the world's most-wanted war criminal. I attended SDS press conferences and listened to Karadžić's roaring paranoia and racism, his imposing head looming on our horizon: large, cuboid, topped with an unruly gray mane. And Professor Koljević would be there too, sitting next to Karadžić: small, solemn, and academic, with large jar-bottom glasses, wearing a tweed jacket with suede elbow patches, his long fingers crossed loosely in front of his face, as if suspended between a prayer and applause. Afterward, I'd come up to greet him, dutifully, assuming that we still shared a love of books. "Stay out of this," he'd advise me. "Stick to literature."

In 1992, when the Serbian attack on Bosnia and the siege of Sarajevo began, I found myself in the United States. Safe in Chicago, I watched Serbian snipers shoot at the knees and ankles of a man trying to escape from a truck that had been hit by a rocket. On the front pages of magazines and news-papers, I saw emaciated prisoners in Serbian camps, and the terrified faces of people running down Sniper Alley. I watched as the Sarajevo library perished in patient, deliberate flames.

The infernal irony of a poet (bad though he may have been) and a literature professor causing the destruction of hundreds of thousands of books did not escape me. On the news, I sometimes caught a glimpse of Professor Koljević standing beside Karadžić, who was always deny-ing something—what was happening was for him either "self-defense" or it was not happening at all. Occasionally, Professor Koljević talked to reporters himself, mocking the questions about rape camps, or deflecting all accusations of Serbian crimes by framing them as the unfortunate things that take place in every "civil war." In Marcel Ophüls's *The Troubles We've Seen*, a documentary about foreign report-ers covering the war in Bosnia, Professor Koljević—labeled as "Serbian Shakespearean"—speaks to a BBC reporter, dis-pensing spin phrases in impeccable English and explaining away the sounds of Serbian shells falling on Sarajevo in the background as a part of the ritual celebration of Orthodox Christmas. "Obviously," he said, "from the old times, Serbs like to do this." He smiled as he said that, apparently relish-ing his own cleverness. "But it is not even Christmas," the BBC reporter observed.

I became obsessed with Professor Koljević. I kept trying to identify the first moment when I could have noticed his genocidal proclivities. Racked with guilt, I recalled his lectures and the conversations we'd had, as if picking through ashes—the ashes of my library. I *unread* books and poems I used to like—from Emily Dickinson to Danilo Kiš, from Frost to Tolstoy—*unlearning* the way in which he had taught me to read them, because I should've known, I should've paid attention. I'd been mired in close reading, impressionable and unaware that my favorite teacher was involved in plotting a vast crime. But what's done cannot be undone.

Now it seems clear to me that his evil had far more influence on me than his literary vision. I excised and exterminated that precious, youthful part of me that had believed you could retreat from history and hide from evil in the comforts of art. Because of Professor Koljević, perhaps, my writing is infused with testy impatience for bourgeois babbling, regrettably tainted with helpless rage I cannot be rid of.

Toward the end of the war, Professor Koljević fell out of favor with Karadžić and was demoted from the realms of power. He spent his time drinking heavily, now and then giving an interview to a foreign journalist, ranting about various injustices committed against the Serbian people in general and himself in particular. In 1997, he blew his Shakespeare-laden brains out. He had to shoot twice, his long piano-player finger apparently having trembled on the unwieldy trigger.

THE LIVES OF A FLANEUR

...

In the spring of 1997, I flew from Chicago, where I was living, to Sarajevo, where I was born. This was my first return
to Sarajevo since the war in Bosnia and Herzegovina had
ended a year and a half before. I'd left a few months before
the siege of the city started. I had no family there (my parents
and my sister now lived in Canada), except for teta-Jozefina,
whom I thought of as my grandmother. When my parents
had moved to Sarajevo after graduating from college in
1963, they'd rented a room in the apartment of Jozefina and
her husband, Martin, in the part of town called Marin dvor.
In that rented room I was conceived, and it was where I lived
for the first two years of my life. Teta-Jozefina and čika-
Martin, who had two teenage children at the time, treated
me as their own grandchild—to this day, my mother believes
that they spoiled me for life. For a couple of years after we'd
moved out to a different part of Sarajevo, I had to be taken

back to Marin dvor to visit them every single day. And until the war shattered our common life, we spent each Christmas at teta-Jozefina and čika-Martin's. Every year, we followed the same ritual: the same elaborately caloric dishes crowding the big table, the same tongue-burning Herzegovinian wine, the same people telling the same jokes and stories, including the one featuring the toddler version of me running up and down the hallway butt-naked before my nightly bath.

Čika-Martin died of a stroke toward the end of the siege, so in 1997 teta-Jozefina was living alone. I stayed with her upon my return, in the room (and, possibly, the very bed) where I'd commenced my exhaustingly messy existence. Its walls were pockmarked by shrapnel and bullets—the apartment had been directly in the sight line of a Serb sniper across the river. Teta-Jozefina was a devout Catholic, but she somehow managed to believe in essential human goodness, despite all the abundant evidence to the contrary surrounding her. She felt that the sniper was essentially a good man because during the siege, she said, he had often shot over her and her husband's heads to warn them that he was watching and that they shouldn't move so carelessly in their own apartment.

In my first few days back in Sarajevo, I did little but listen to teta-Jozefina's harrowing and humbling stories of the siege, including a detailed rendition of her husband's death (where he had sat, what he had said, how he had slumped), and wander around the city. I was trying to reconcile the new Sarajevo with the 1992 version I'd left for America. It wasn't easy for me to comprehend how the siege had transformed the city, because the transformation wasn't as simple as one thing becoming another. Everything was fantastically different from what I'd known and everything was fantastically the same as before. Our old room (and, possibly, bed) was the same; the buildings stood in the same places; the bridges crossed the river at the same points; the streets followed the same obscure yet familiar logic; the layout of the city was unaltered. But the room had been marred by siege scars; the buildings had been mutilated by shells and shrapnel showers, or reduced to crumbling walls; the river had been the front line, so some of the bridges were destroyed and much in their vicinity was leveled; the streets were fractured by mortar-shell marks—lines radiating from a little crater at the point of impact—which an art group had filled out with red paint and which the people of Sarajevo now, incredibly, called "roses."

I revisited all my favorite spots in the city center, then roamed the narrow streets high up in the hills, beyond which lay a verdant world of unmapped minefields. I randomly entered building hallways and basements, just to smell them: in addition to the familiar scent of leather suitcases, old magazines, and damp coal dust, there was the smell of hard life and sewage—during the siege, people had taken shelter from the shelling in their basements. I idled in coffee shops, drinking coffee that tasted unlike what I remembered from before the war—it was like burnt corn now. As a Bosnian in

Chicago, I'd experienced one form of displacement, but this was another: I was displaced in a place that had been mine. In Sarajevo, everything around me was familiar to the point of pain and entirely uncanny and distant.

One day I was strolling, aimlessly and anxiously, down the street whose prewar name had been Ulica JNA (The Yugoslav People's Army Street) and now was Ulica Branilaca Sarajeva (The Defenders of Sarajevo Street). As I walked past what had been called, in the heady times of socialism—which now seemed positively prehistoric—the Workers' University (Radnički univerzitet), something made me turn and look over my shoulder into its cavernous entranceway. The turn was not of my own volition: it was my body that spun my head back, while my mind went on for a few steps. Impeding impatient pedestrian traffic, I stood puzzled before the late Workers' University until I realized what had made me look back: the Workers' University used to house a movie theater (it had shut down a couple of years before the war), and whenever I'd walked by in those days, I'd looked at the display cases where the posters and show times were exhibited. From the lightless shafts of corporal memory, my body had recalled the action of turning to see what was playing. It had been trained to react to urban stimulation in the form of a new movie poster, and it still remembered, the fucker, the way it remembered how to swim when thrown into deep water. Following that involuntary revolution, my mind was flooded with a banal, if Proustian, memory: once upon a time in Sarajevo, at the Workers' University, I'd watched

Sergio Leone's *Once upon a Time in America*, and now I recalled the pungent smell of the disinfectant that was used to clean the floors of the cinema; I recalled peeling myself off the sticky fake-leather seats; I recalled the rattle of the parting curtain.

I'd left Sarajevo for America on January 24, 1992. I had no way of knowing at the time that I'd return to my hometown only as an irreversibly displaced visitor. I was twenty-seven (and a half) and had never lived anywhere else, nor had any desire to do so. I'd spent the few years before the trip working as a journalist in what was known, in socialist, peacetime Yugoslavia, as the "youth press" (*omladinska štampa*), generally less constrained than the mainstream press, reared in the pressure chamber of Tito's one-party state. My last paid job was for *Naši dani*, where I edited the culture pages. (Before the war, the domain of *culture* seemed to offer a haven from the increasingly hateful world of politics. Now, when I hear the word *culture*, I pull out the quote commonly attributed to Hermann Göring: "When I hear the word *culture*, I reach for my revolver.") I wrote film reviews but was far better known for my column "Sarajevo Republika." The name was intended as an allusion to the Mediterranean Renaissance city-states—Dubrovnik or Venice—as well as to the slogan "*Kosovo republika*," which had been sprayed on Kosovo walls by the "irredentists," who demanded that Kosovo be given the status of a republic in the federal

Yugoslavia; given full sovereignty, that is, in place of its status as an "autonomous province" of Serbia. In other words, I was a militant Sarajevan. I set out in my column to assert Sarajevo's uniqueness, the inherent sovereignty of its spirit, reproducing and extolling its urban mythology in a prose arrogantly thick with abstruse Sarajevo slang. The first column I ever published was about an *aščinica*—a traditional Bosnian storefront restaurant, serving cooked (as opposed to grilled) food—which had been run by a local family, the Hadžibajrićs, for a hundred and fifty years or so. One of the urban legends about the Hadžibajrićs claimed that, back in the seventies, during the shooting of the movie *The Battle of Sutjeska*, a state-produced Second World War spectacle, starring Richard Burton as Tito, a Yugoslav People's Army helicopter was frequently deployed to the set deep in the mountains of eastern Bosnia, to transport the Hadžibajrićs' *buredžici* (meat pies in sour cream) for Elizabeth Taylor's gastronomic enjoyment. To this day, many of us are proud of the possibility that some of the fat in Purple Eyes's ass came from Sarajevo.

The columns that followed were about the philosophy of Sarajevo's baroque slang; about the myriad time-wasting strategies I believed were essential for urban-mythology (re)production, and which I executed daily in innumerable *kafana*s; about bingo venues, frequented by habitual losers, bottom-feeders, and young urbanites in pursuit of coolness credentials. One of the columns was about the main pedestrian thoroughfare in the heart of the city—Vase Miskina Street (known as Ferhadija since the fluttering fall of socialism)—which stretched from downtown to the old town. I referred to it as the city artery, because many Sarajevans promenaded along it at least twice a day, keeping the urban circulation going. If you spent enough time drinking coffee at one of the many *kafana*s along Vase Miskina, the whole city would eventually parade past you. In the early nineties, street peddlers stationed themselves along the street, pushing the penny-cheap detritus of the wrecked workers' state: sewing-machine needles, screwdrivers, and Russian–Serbo-Croat dictionaries. These days, it is all Third World–capitalism junk: pirated DVDs, made-in-China plastic toys, herbal remedies and miraculous sexual enhancers.

Fancying myself a street-savvy columnist, I raked the city for material, absorbing details and generating ideas. I don't know if I would've used the word back then, but now I'm prone to reimagining my young self as one of Baudelaire's flaneurs, as someone who wanted to be everywhere and nowhere in particular, for whom wandering in the city was the main means of communication with it. Sarajevo was—and still is—a small town, viscous with stories and history, brimming with people I knew and loved, all of whom I could monitor from a well-chosen *kafana* perch or by patrolling the streets. As I surveyed the estuaries of Vase Miskina or the obscure, narrow streets creeping up the hills, complete paragraphs flooded my brain; not infrequently, and mysteriously, a simple lust would possess my body. The city laid itself down for me; wandering stimulated my body as well as my mind. It probably didn't hurt that my daily caffeine intake bordered on stroke-inducing—what wine and opium must've been for Baudelaire, coffee and cigarettes were for me.

As I would in 1997, I entered buildings just to smell their hallways. I studied the edges of stone stairs blunted by the many soles that had rubbed against them over the past century or two. I spent time at the Željo soccer stadium, deserted on a gameless day, eavesdropping on the pensioners—the retirees who were lifelong season-ticket holders—as they strolled within its walls in nostalgic circles, discussing the heartrending losses and unlikely victories of the past. I returned to places I'd known my whole life so that I could experience them differently and capture details that had been blurred by excessive familiarity. I collected sensations and faces, smells and sights, fully internalizing Sarajevo's architecture and physiognomies. I gradually became aware that my interiority was inseparable from my exteriority. Physically and metaphysically, I was *placed*. If my friends spotted me on a side street looking up at the high friezes typical of Austro-Hungarian architecture, or lingering on a lonely park bench, watching dogs fetch and couples make out—the kind of behavior that might have seemed worrisome—they just assumed that I was working on a column. Most likely, I was.

Despite my grand plans, I ended up writing only six or seven "Sarajevo Republika" columns before *Naši dani* ran its course out of money. The magazine's dissolution was inconspicuous within the ongoing dissolution of Yugoslavia.

In the summer of 1991, incidents in the neighboring Croatia developed into a full-fledged fast-spreading war while rumors persisted that the army was secretly transferring troops and weapons to the parts of Bosnia with a majority Serb population. *Oslobodjenje*, the Sarajevo daily paper, got hold of a military plan outlining troop redeployment in Bosnia and Herzegovina that clearly suggested the imminence of war, even though the army firmly denied the plan.

The army spokespeople weren't the only ones denying the blatant likelihood of war—the urbanites of Sarajevo were also intent on ignoring the obvious, if for different reasons. In the summer of 1991 parties, sex, and drugs were abundant; the laughter was hysterical; the streets seemed packed day and night. In the seductive glow of inevitable catastrophe, the city appeared more beautiful than ever. By early September, however, the complicated operations of denial were hopelessly winding down. When I wandered the city, I found myself speculating with troubling frequency as to which buildings would provide good sniper positions. Even as I envisioned myself ducking under fire, I took those visions to be simply paranoid symptoms of the stress induced by the ubiquitous warmongering politics. I understand now that I was imagining *incidents*, as it was hard for me to imagine *war* in all its force, much the way a young person can imagine the symptoms of an illness but find it hard to imagine death: life seems so continuously, intensely, and undeniably present.

Nowadays in Sarajevo, death is all too easy to imagine

and is continuously, undeniably present, but back then the city—a beautiful, immortal thing, an indestructible republic of urban spirit—was fully alive both inside and outside me. Its indelible sensory dimension, its concreteness, seemed to defy the abstractions of war. I have learned since then that war is the most concrete thing there can be, a fantastic reality that levels both interiority and exteriority into the flatness of a crushed soul.

One day in the early summer of 1991, I went to the American Cultural Center in Sarajevo for the interview that was supposed to determine my suitability for the International Visitors Program, a cultural exchange run by the now defunct United States Information Agency—which I hoped was a spy outfit whose employees went undercover as culture lovers. Even being considered for an invitation to America was flattering, of course, because you had to be deaf, dumb, blind, and comatose to avoid American culture in the Sarajevo of my youth. By the time I graduated from high school, in 1983, my favorite movie of all time was Coppola's *Apocalypse Now*. I worshipped Patti Smith, Talking Heads, and Television, and CBGB was to me what Jerusalem must be to a devout believer. I often imitated Holden Caulfield's diction (in translation) and once manipulated my unwitting father into buying a Bukowski book for my birthday. By the time I graduated from college, in 1990, I could act out with my sister chunks of dialogue (mispronounced) from *His*

Girl Friday. I'd get angry at people who couldn't recognize the genius of Brian De Palma. I could recite Public Enemy's angry invectives, and was up to my ears in Sonic Youth and Swans. I piously read American short-story anthologies, available in translation, in which Barth and Barthelme reigned. I hadn't really read Barth's famous essay, but I thought that the notion of the literature of exhaustion was very cool. I wrote an essay on Bret Easton Ellis and corporate capitalism.

I met the man in charge of the center, chitted and chatted about this and that (mainly that), and then went home. I didn't think that my visit to America would ever come to pass, nor had I noticed the man actually evaluating me. Despite my fondness for American culture, I didn't care all that much. Even if I thought it would be fun to Kerouac about in America for a while, I had no particular desire to leave Sarajevo. I loved my city; I intended to tell stories about it to my children and my grandchildren, to grow old and die there. Around that time, I was having a passionate on-and-off relationship with a young woman who was working hard to get out of Sarajevo and move abroad because, she said, she felt that she didn't belong there. "It's not about where you belong, it's about what belongs to you," I told her, possibly quoting from some movie or another. I was twenty-seven (and a half) and Sarajevo belonged to me.

I'd pretty much forgotten about my summer chitchat when, in early December, I received a call from the American Cultural Center inviting me for a monthlong visit to the

United States. By that time I was exhausted by the onslaught of warmongering, and I accepted the invitation. I thought that being away would provide some relief. I planned to travel around the States for a month, then, before returning to Sarajevo, visit an old friend in Chicago. I landed at O'Hare on March 14, 1992. I remember that day as vast, clear, and sunny. On my way in from the airport I saw for the first time the skyline of Chicago—an enormous, distant, geometrical city, less emerald than dark against the blue firmament.

By this time, the Yugoslav People's Army's troops were fully deployed all over Bosnia, following the previously denied plan; Serbian paramilitaries were crazy-busy slaughtering; there were random barricades and shootings on the streets of Sarajevo. In early April, a peaceful demonstration in front of the Bosnian Parliament building was targeted by Karadžić's snipers. Two women were killed on the Vrbanja Bridge, a hundred yards or so from teta-Jozefina's apartment, quite conceivably by the same good sniper who later maculated the walls in the room of my conception. On the outskirts of the city, in the hills above, the war was already mature and raging, but in the heart of Sarajevo people still seemed to think that it would somehow stop before it reached them. To my worried inquiries from Chicago, my mother would respond, "There is already less shooting than yesterday"—as though war were a spring shower.

My father, however, advised me to stay away. Nothing good was going to happen at home, he said. I was supposed to fly back from Chicago on May 1, and as things got progressively worse in Sarajevo, I was torn between guilt and fear for my parents' and friends' lives, kept awake by worries about my previously unimagined and presently unimaginable future in America. I wrangled with my conscience: if you were the author of a column entitled "Sarajevo Republika" then it was perhaps your duty to go back and defend your city and its spirit from annihilation.

Much of that wrangling I did while incessantly roaming Chicago, as though I could simply walk off my moral anxiety. I'd pick a movie that I wanted to see—both for distraction and out of my old habits as a film reviewer—then locate, with my friend's help, a theater that was showing it. From Ukrainian Village, the neighborhood where I was staying, I'd take public transportation to buy a ticket a couple of hours before the show and then I'd wander in concentric circles around the movie theater. My first journey was to the Esquire (now no longer a movie venue) on Oak Street, in the affluent Gold Coast neighborhood—the Esquire was my Plymouth Rock. The movie was Michael Apted's *Thunderheart*, in which Val Kilmer played an FBI agent of Native American background who pursues a case to a reservation, which somehow forces him to come to terms with his past and heritage. I remember the movie being as bad as it now sounds, though I don't remember many details. Nor do I remember much of my first Gold Coast roam, because it has become indistinguishable from all the other ones, the way the first day of school is subsumed in the entirety of your educational experience.

I subsequently journeyed to movie theaters all over Chicago and walked in circles around them. I saw more bad movies in so-called bad neighborhoods, where, the movies notwithstanding, nothing bad ever happened to me. There was always plenty of space for walking, as few cared to crowd the streets in those parts of Chicago. When I had no money for the movies—my main source of income was the card game Preference, which I had taught my friend and his buddies to play—I would explore the cinema-free areas of Wicker Park, Bucktown, or Humboldt Park (Saul Bellow's childhood neighborhood), which was adjacent to Ukrainian Village and, I was warned, gang-infested.

I couldn't quit. A tormented flaneur, I kept walking, my Achilles tendons sore, my head in the clouds of fear and longing for Sarajevo, until I finally reconciled myself to the idea of staying. On May 1, I didn't fly home. On May 2, the roads out of the city were blocked; the last train (with my parents on it) departed; the longest siege in modern history began. In Chicago, I submitted my application for political asylum. The rest is the rest of my life.

In my ambulatory expeditions, I became acquainted with Chicago, but I didn't *know* the city. The need to know it in my body, to locate myself in the world, wasn't satisfied; I was metaphysically ailing, because I didn't yet know how to *be* in Chicago. The American city was organized fundamentally differently from Sarajevo. (A few years later I would find a Bellow quote that perfectly encapsulated my feeling of the city at the time: "Chicago was nowhere. It had no setting. It was something released into American space.") Where the urban landscapes of Sarajevo had been populated with familiar faces, with shared and shareable experiences, the Chicago I was trying to comprehend was dark with the matter of pursued anonymity.

In Sarajevo, you possessed a personal infrastructure: your *kafana*, your barber, your butcher; the streets where people recognized you, the space that identified you; the landmarks of your life (the spot where you fell playing soccer and broke your arm, the corner where you waited to meet the first of the many loves of your life, the bench where you kissed her first). Because anonymity was well nigh impossible and privacy literally incomprehensible (there is no word for "privacy" in Bosnian), your fellow Sarajevans knew you as well as you knew them. The borders between interiority and exteriority were practically nonexistent. If you somehow vanished, your fellow citizens could have collectively reconstructed you from their collective memory and the gossip accrued over the years. Your sense of who you were, your deepest identity, was determined by your position in a human network, whose physical corollary was the architecture of the city. Chicago, on the other hand, was built not for people to come together but for them to be safely apart. Size, power, and the need for privacy seemed to be the dominant dimensions of its architecture. Vast as it is, Chicago ignored the distinctions between freedom and isolation, between independence and selfishness, between privacy and loneliness. In this city, I had no human network within which I could place myself; my Sarajevo, the city that had existed inside me and was still there, was subject to siege and destruction. My displacement was metaphysical to the precisely same extent to which it was physical. But I couldn't live nowhere; I wanted from Chicago what I'd got from Sarajevo: a geography of the soul.

More walking was needed, as was, even more pressingly, reasonably gainful employment. Nothing in my experience had taught me how to get a job in America. Neither De Palma's oeuvre nor the literature of exhaustion contained any pointers about getting urgently needed work. After a few illegal, below-minimum-wage jobs, some of which required me to furnish someone else's Social Security number (fuck you, Arizona!), I received my work permit and entered the crowded minimum-wage labor market. For restaurant managers and people in temp agencies looking for bouncers and bartenders, I created a vast and partly false universe of my previous life, at the center of which was a familiarity with all things American. They couldn't care less; it took me a few weeks to learn that (a) rambling about American movies could not even get you a most penurious job; and (b) when they say "We'll call you!" they don't really mean it.

My first legal job was canvassing door-to-door for Greenpeace, an organization inherently welcoming to misfits. When I first called the Greenpeace office to inquire, I didn't even know what the job was, what the word *canvassing* meant. Naturally, I was terrified of talking to Americans on their doorsteps, what with my insufficient English, devoid of articles and thickly contaminated with a foreign accent, but I craved the ambulatory freedom between the doors. So, in the early summer of 1992, I found myself canvassing in the proudly indistinguishable, dull western suburbs (Schaumburg, Naperville); in the wealthy North Shore ones (Wilmette, Winnetka, Lake Forest), with their hospital-size houses and herds of cars in palatial garages; in the southern working-class ones (Blue Island, Park Forest), where people invited me into their homes and offered me stale Twinkies. Soon I learned to assess the annual income and political leanings of the household based on the look of the lawn, the magazines in the mailbox, and the makes of the family vehicles (Volvo meant liberal). I enabled myself to endure questions about Bosnia and Yugoslavia and their nonexistent relation to the nonexistent Czechoslovakia. I grinned through lectures on the spirituality of *Star Trek* and confirmed, calmly, that, yes, I had been exposed in Sarajevo to the wonders of pizza and television. I smiled at a young man who implored me to understand how broke he was, as he had just bought a Porsche. I had lemonade at the home of a soft-spoken Catholic priest and his young, gorgeous boyfriend, who was bored and tipsy. I sought shelter with a couple who had a beautiful Alphonse Mucha print on the wall, after their neighbor had shown me his gun and his willingness to use it. I discussed helmet laws with a herd of pot-bellied balding bikers, some of them veterans who believed that what they had fought for in Vietnam was the freedom to spill their brains on the freeways of America. I witnessed African American fellow canvassers being repeatedly stopped by the police protecting their quaint suburban domain.

My favorite turf was, predictably, in the city: Pullman, Beverly, Lakeview, and then the Parks—Hyde, Lincoln, Rogers. Little by little, I began to sort out the geography of Chicagoland, assembling a street map in my mind, building by building, door by door. Occasionally, I took my time before canvassing and slacked off in a local diner, struggling to enjoy the burnt-corn taste of American coffee, monitoring the foot traffic, the corner drug trade, the friendly ladies. Every once in a while, I skipped work entirely and just walked and walked in the neighborhood assigned to me. I was a low-wage, immigrant flaneur.

At the same time, I was obsessively following TV reports from the besieged Sarajevo, trying to identify people and places on the screen, to assess from afar the extent of the devastation. Toward the end of May, I watched the footage of a massacre on Vase Miskina, where a Serb shell hit a bread line, killing scores of Sarajevans. I attempted to identify the people on the screen—writhing in a puddle of rose-red blood, their legs torn off, their faces distorted with shock—but I couldn't. I had a hard time recognizing the place as well. The street I'd thought I owned, and had frivolously dubbed the city artery, was now awash in the actual arterial blood of those I'd left behind, and all I could do was watch the looping thirty-second stories on *Headline News*.

Even from Chicago, I could guess at the magnitude of my hometown's transformation. The street that connected my neighborhood (Socijalno) with downtown was rechristened Sniper Alley. The Željo stadium, where I'd eavesdropped on the pensioners, was now controlled by the Serbs, its wooden stands burned down. The little bakery in Kovači that produced the best *somun* (leavened pita bread) in town, and therefore in the world, was also burned down. The Museum of the 1984 Winter Olympic Games, housed in a beautiful Austro-Hungarian building of no strategic value whatsoever, was shelled (and is still a ruin). The pseudo-Moorish National Library was shelled; along with its hundreds of thousands of books, it burned down.

In December 1994, I briefly volunteered at the International Human Rights Law Institute of DePaul University's College of Law, where evidence of possible war crimes in Bosnia was being collected. By then, I'd quit canvassing and enrolled in graduate school at Northwestern, and I desperately needed another job, so I showed up at the institute's downtown office, hoping that they would give me one. There was no way for my prospective employers to know who I was or had been—I could easily have been a spy—so they offered me what they thought were simple volunteer tasks. At first, I did some data input for the concentration-camp database, where every testimony or mention of a camp was filed. But eventually I was given a stack of photos of destroyed and damaged buildings in Sarajevo, as yet unidentified, and asked to note their locations. Many of the buildings photographed were roofless, hole-ridden, or burned, their windows blown out. There were few people in those pictures, but what I was doing felt very much like identifying corpses. Now and then I could recall the street or even the exact address; sometimes the buildings were so familiar they seemed unreal. There was, for example, the building at the corner of Danijela Ozme and Kralja Tomislava, across from which I used to wait for Renata, my high school girlfriend, to come down from Džidžikovac. Back then, there was a supermarket on the ground floor of the building, where I'd buy candy or cigarettes when she was late, which was always. I'd known that building for years. It had stood in its place solid, indelible. I'd never devoted any thought to it until I saw its picture in Chicago. In the photograph, the building was hollow, disemboweled by a shell, which had evidently fallen through the roof and dropped down a few floors. The supermarket now existed only in the flooded storage space of my memory.

There were also buildings that I recognized but could not exactly place. And then there were the ones that were wholly unknown to me—I couldn't even figure out what part of town they might have been in. I have learned since then that you don't need to know every part of a city to own the whole of it, but in that office in downtown Chicago it terrified me to think that there was some part of Sarajevo I didn't know and probably never would, as it was now disintegrating, like a cardboard stage set, in the rain of shells. If my mind and my city were the same thing then I was losing my mind. Converting Chicago into my personal space became not just metaphysically essential but psychiatrically urgent as well.

In the spring of 1993, after a year or so of living in Ukrainian Village, I moved to a lakeside neighborhood called Edgewater, on Chicago's North Side. I rented a tiny studio in a building called Artists in Residence, in which various lonely and not exactly successful artists resided. The AiR provided a loose sense of community within the city's anonymity; it offered a rehearsal space for musicians, dancers, and actors, as well as a public computer for those of us who harbored writerly hopes. The building manager's implausibly appropriate name was Art.

Back then, Edgewater was where one went to acquire cheap—and bad—heroin. I'd been warned that it was a rough neighborhood, but what I saw there were varieties of despair that exactly matched my own. One day I stood on Winthrop Avenue looking up at the top of a building on whose ledge a young woman sat deliberating whether to kill herself, while a couple of guys down on the street kept shouting, "Jump!" They did so out of sheer asshole malice, of course, but at the time their suggestion seemed to me a reasonable resolution to the continuous problem we call life.

I was still working as a canvasser for Greenpeace, walking different city neighborhoods and suburbs every day, already becoming far too familiar with many of them. But every night I came back to the Edgewater studio I could call my own, where I was beginning to develop a set of ritualistic, comforting practices. Before sleep, I'd listen to a demented monologue delivered by a chemically stimulated corner loiterer, occasionally muffled by the soothing sound of trains clattering past on the El tracks. In the morning, drinking coffee, I'd watch from my window the people waiting at the Granville El stop, recognizing the regulars. I'd occasionally splurge on breakfast at a Shoney's on Broadway (now long gone) that offered a $2.99 all-you-can-eat deal to the likes of me and the drooling residents of a nursing home on Winthrop, who would arrive en masse, holding hands like schoolchildren. At Gino's North, where there was only one beer on tap and where many an artist got shitfaced, I'd watch the victorious Bulls' games, high-fiving only the select company of those who were not too drunk to lift their elbows off the bar. I'd spend weekends playing chess at a Rogers Park coffee shop, next to a movie theater. I often played with an old Assyrian named Peter, who, whenever he put me in an indefensible position and I offered to resign, would crack the same joke: "Can I have that in writing?" But there was no writing coming from me. Deeply displaced, I could write neither in Bosnian nor in English.

Little by little, people in Edgewater began to recognize me; I started greeting them on the street. Over time, I acquired a barber and a butcher and a movie theater and a coffee shop with a steady set of colorful characters—which were, as I'd learned in Sarajevo, the necessary knots in any personal urban network. I discovered that the process of transforming an American city into a space you could call your own required starting in a particular neighborhood. Soon I began to claim Edgewater as mine; I became a local. It was there that I understood what Nelson Algren meant when he wrote that loving Chicago was like loving a woman with a broken nose—I fell in love with the broken noses of Edgewater. On the AiR's ancient communal Mac, I typed my first attempts at stories in English.

Therefore it was of utmost significance that Edgewater turned out to be the neighborhood where shiploads of Bosnians escaping the war ended up in the spring of 1994. I experienced a shock of recognition one day when I looked out my window and saw a family strolling down the street—where few ever walked, except in pursuit of heroin—in an unmistakably Bosnian formation: the eldest male member leading the way, at a slow, aimless pace, hands on their butts, all of them slouching, as though burdened by a weighty load of worries. Before long, the neighborhood was dense with Bosnians. Contrary to the local customs, they took evening walks, the anxiety of displacement clear in their step; in large, silent groups, they drank coffee at a lakeside Turkish café (thereby converting it into a proper *kafana*), a dark cloud of war trauma and cigarette smoke hovering over them; their children played on the street, oblivious to the drug business conducted on the corner. I could monitor them now from my window, from the *kafana*, on the street. It was as if they had come looking for me in Edgewater.

In February 1997, a couple of months before my first return to Sarajevo, Veba came to Chicago for a visit; I hadn't seen him since my departure. For the first few days, I listened to his stories of life under siege, the stories of horrible transformation the war had forced upon the besieged. I was still living at the AiR. Despite the February cold, Veba wanted to see where my life was taking place, so we wandered around Edgewater: to the Shoney's, the chess café, the *kafana* on the now-iced-over lake. He got a haircut at my barber's; we bought meat at my butcher's. I told him my Edgewater stories: about the young woman on the ledge, about the Bosnian family walking in formation, about Peter the Assyrian.

Then we ventured out of Edgewater to visit Ukrainian Village, and I showed him where I'd lived; I took him to the Burger King where I'd fattened myself into American shape while listening to old Ukes discussing Ukrainian politics over sixty-nine-cent coffee—I used to call them the Knights of the Burger King. We wandered around the Gold Coast, spotting a Matisse in some rich person's apartment, nicely positioned so that it could be seen from the street; we saw a movie at the Esquire. We visited the Water Tower and I spoke about the great Chicago fire. We had a drink at the Green Mill, where Al Capone used to imbibe martinis, and where every giant of jazz, from Louis Armstrong to Charlie Mingus, had performed. I showed him where the St. Valentine's Day massacre had taken place: the garage was long gone, but the urban myth had it that dogs still growled when walking past, as they could smell the blood.

Showing Veba around, telling him the stories of Chicago and of my life in Edgewater, I realized that my immigrant interior had begun to merge with the American exterior. Large parts of Chicago had entered me and settled there; I fully owned those parts now. I saw Chicago through the eyes of Sarajevo and the two cities now created a complicated internal landscape in which stories could be generated. When I came back from my first visit to Sarajevo, in the spring of 1997, the Chicago I came back to belonged to me. Returning from home, I returned home.

REASONS WHY I DO NOT WISH TO LEAVE CHICAGO: AN INCOMPLETE, RANDOM LIST

■ ■ ■

1. Driving west at sunset in the summer: blinded by the sun, you cannot see the cars ahead; the ugly warehouses and body shops are blazing orange. When the sun sets, everything becomes deeper: the brick facades acquire a bluish hue; there are charcoal smudges of darkness on the horizon. The sky and the city look endless. West is everywhere you look.

2. The way people in the winter huddle together under the warming lights on the Granville El stop, much like young chickens under a lightbulb. It is an image of human solidarity enforced by the cruelty of nature, the story of Chicago and of civilization.

3. The American vastness of the Wilson Street beach, gulls and kites coasting above it, dogs sprinting along the jagged waves, barking into the void, city kids doing

homemade drugs, blind to the distant ships on their mysterious ways from Liverpool, England, to Gary, Indiana.

4. Early September anyplace in the city, when the sunlight angles have abruptly changed and everything and everyone appears better, all the edges softened; the torments of the hot summer are now over, the cold torments of the winter have not begun, and people bask in the perishable possibility of a kind and gentle city.

5. The basketball court at Foster Street beach, where I once watched an impressively sculpted guy play a whole game—dribbling, shooting, arguing, dunking—with a toothpick in his mouth, taking it out only to spit. For many years he was to me the hero of Chicago cool.

6. The tall ice ranges along the shore when the winter is exceptionally cold and the lake frozen for a while, so ice pushes ice against the land. One freezing day I stood there in awe, realizing that the process exactly replicates the way mountain ranges were formed hundreds of millions of years ago, tectonic plates pushing against each other. The primeval shapes are visible to every cranky driver plowing through the Lake Shore Drive mess, but most of them look ahead and couldn't care less.

7. Looking directly west at night from any Edgewater or Rogers Park high-rise: airplanes hover and glimmer above O'Hare. Once, my visiting mother and I spent an entire evening sitting in the dark, listening to Frank Sinatra, watching the planes, which resembled stunned fire-

flies, transfixed with the continuous wonder that this world is.

8. The blessed scarcity of celebrities in Chicago, most of whom are overpaid athlete losers. Oprah, one of the Friends, and many other people whose names I never knew or now cannot recall have all left for New York or Hollywood or rehab, where they can wear the false badge of their humble Chicago roots, while we can claim them without actually being responsible for the vacuity of their front-page lives.

9. The Hyde Park parakeets, miraculously surviving brutal winters, a colorful example of life that adamantly refuses to perish, of the kind of instinct that has made Chicago harsh and great. I actually have never seen one: the possibility that they are made-up makes the whole thing even better.

10. The downtown skyline at night as seen from the Adler Planetarium: lit windows within the dark building frames the darker sky. It seems that stars have been squared and pasted on the thick wall of a Chicago night; the cold, inhuman beauty containing the enormity of life, each window a possible story, inside which an immigrant is putting in a late shift cleaning corporate trash.

11. The green-gray color of the barely foaming lake when the winds are northwesterly and the sky is chilly.

12. The summer days, long and humid, when the streets seem waxed with sweat; when the air is as thick and

warm as honey-sweetened tea; when the beaches are full of families: fathers barbecuing, mothers sunbathing, children approaching hypothermia in the lake's shallows. Then a wave of frigid air sweeps the parks, a diluvial shower soaks every living creature, and someone, somewhere loses power. (Never trust a summer day in Chicago.)

13. The highly muggable suburbanites patrolling Michigan Avenue, identifiable by their Hard Rock Café shirts, oblivious to the city beyond the shopping and entertainment areas; the tourists on an architectural speedboat tour looking up at the steep buildings like pirates ready to plunder; the bridges' halves symmetrically erected like jousting pricks; the street performer in front of the Wrigley Building performing "Killing Me Softly" on the tuba.

14. The fact that every year in March, the Cubs fans start saying: "This year might be it!"—a delusion betrayed as such by the time summer arrives, when the Cubs traditionally lose even a mathematical possibility of making it to the play-offs. The hopeless hope is one of the early harbingers of spring, bespeaking an innocent belief that the world might right its wrongs and reverse its curses simply because the trees are coming into leaf.

15. A warm February day when everyone present at my butcher shop discussed the distinct possibility of a perfect snowstorm and, in turn, remembered the great snowstorm of 1967: cars abandoned and buried in snow

on Lake Shore Drive; people trudging home from work through the blizzard like refugees; the snow on your street up to the milk truck's mirrors. There are a lot of disasters in the city's memory, which result in a strangely euphoric nostalgia, somehow akin to a Chicagoan's respect for and pride in "those four-mansion crooks who risk their lives in crimes of high visibility" (Bellow).

16. Pakistani and Indian families strolling solemnly up and down Devon on summer evenings; Russian Jewish senior couples clustering on Uptown benches, warbling gossip in soft consonants against the blare of obsolete transistor radios; Mexican families in Pilsen crowding Nuevo Leon for Sunday breakfast; African American families gloriously dressed for church, waiting for a table in the Hyde Park Dixie Kitchen; Somali refugees playing soccer in sandals on the Senn High School pitch; young Bucktown mothers carrying yoga mats on their backs like bazookas; the enormous amount of daily life in this city, much of it worth a story or two.

17. A river of red and a river of white flowing in opposite directions on Lake Shore Drive, as seen from Montrose Harbor at night.

18. The wind: the sailboats in Grant Park Harbor bobbing on the water, the mast wires hysterically clucking; the Buckingham Fountain's upward stream turned into a water plume; the windows of downtown buildings shaking and thumping; people walking down Michigan Avenue with their heads retracted between their

shoulders; my street completely deserted except for a bundled-up mailman and a plastic bag fluttering in the barren tree-crown like a torn flag.

19. The stately Beverly mansions; the bleak Pullman row houses; the frigid buildings of the La Salle Street canyon; the garish beauty of old downtown hotels; the stern arrogance of the Sears Tower and the Hancock Center; the quaint Edgewater houses; the sadness of the West Side; the decrepit grandeur of the Uptown theaters and hotels; the Northwest Side warehouses and body shops; thousands of empty lots and vanished buildings no one pays any attention to and no one will ever remember. Every building tells part of the story of the city. Only the city knows the whole story.

20. If Chicago was good enough for Studs Terkel to spend a lifetime in it, it is good enough for me.

IF GOD EXISTED, HE'D BE A SOLID MIDFIELDER

∎ ∎ ∎

FIRST, A LITTLE BIT ABOUT ME, THOUGH I AM NOT IMPORTANT HERE

By Bosnian standards, I'd been an athletic person. Even though I'd for years smoked a pack and a half a day, had started enjoying alcoholic potions at the ripe age of fifteen, and was fully dependent on a red-meat-and-fat diet, I'd played soccer on the gravel and parking lots of Sarajevo once or twice a week since time immemorial. But soon after my landing in Chicago, I gained weight due to nutrition based on Whoppers and Twinkies, exacerbated by a series of torturous attempts to quit smoking. Furthermore, I couldn't find anybody to play with. My Greenpeace friends deemed rolling joints as physical exercise and only occasionally arranged a lazy softball game, where no score was kept and everyone was always doing great. I couldn't get past understanding the rules, but I did stubbornly try to keep score.

Not playing soccer tormented me. I didn't really care about being healthy as I was still young enough—for me playing soccer was closely related to being fully alive. Without soccer, I felt at sea, mentally and physically. One Saturday in the summer of 1995, I was riding my bike by a lakeside field in Chicago's Uptown and saw people warming up, kicking the ball around while waiting for the game to start. It seemed they might have been getting ready for a league game, for which you had to have registered as a member of a team. But before I had time to consider the humiliating prospect of rejection, I asked if I could join them. Sure, they said, and I kicked the ball for the first time after an eternity of three years. That day I finally played, twenty-five pounds heavier, wearing denim cutoffs and basketball shoes. In no time I pulled my groin and quickly earned blisters on my soles. I humbly played defense (although I'd preferred to play as a forward) and strictly obeyed the commands of the best and fastest player on my team—one Phillip, who had been, I'd learn later, on the Nigerian 4×400 relay team at the Seoul Olympics. After the game, I asked Phillip if I could come back. Ask that guy, Phillip said, and pointed at the ref. The ref wore a striped black-and-white shirt and introduced himself as German. He told me there was a game every Saturday and Sunday and I could always come.

German was not in fact German—he was from Ecuador, but his father was born in Germany, hence his name (Hermann) and nickname. He worked as a UPS truck driver, and was in his mid-forties, suntanned, wearing a modest pompadour and a mustache. Every Saturday and Sunday, he'd arrive by the lake around 2:00 p.m. in a decrepit, twenty-some-year-old van, on which a soccer ball and the words "Kick me make my day" were painted. He'd unload goalposts (made from plastic pipes) and nets, bagfuls of single-color T-shirts, and balls. He'd distribute the shirts to the guys who came to play, put a board on the garbage can, and, on top of it, a number of cheap cups and trophies, little flags of different countries, and a radio blaring Spanish-language stations. Most of the players lived in Uptown and Edgewater and came from Mexico, Honduras, El Salvador, Peru, Chile, Colombia, Belize, Brazil, Jamaica, Nigeria, Somalia, Ethiopia, Senegal, Eritrea, Ghana, Cameroon, Morocco, Algeria, Jordan, France, Spain, Romania, Bulgaria, Bosnia, USA, Ukraine, Russia, France, Vietnam, Korea, et cetera. There was even a guy from Tibet, and he was a very good goalie.

Normally, there'd be more than two teams, and they all had to rotate, so each game lasted for fifteen minutes or until one team scored two goals. The games were very serious and contentious, as the winning team stayed on the field for the next game, while the losing one had to wait on the sidelines for its turn to come back on. German refereed and he almost never called a foul. He'd follow the game with glazed eyes, as though watching soccer made him high; it seemed he needed to hear the sound of a breaking bone to use his whistle. Sometimes, if a team was a player short, he'd referee and play simultaneously. In such a situation, he was particularly hard on himself and once gave himself a yellow card for a rough tackle. We—immigrants trying to stay afloat in this country—found comfort in playing by the rules we set ourselves. It made us feel that we still were a part of the world much bigger than the USA. People acquired their nicknames based on their country of origin. For a while, I was Bosnia, and would often find myself playing in the midfield with, say, Colombia and Romania.

Ever hurting to play and fearing that I'd be left out if I was late, I'd often be the first one to arrive before games. I'd help German set up the goals and then hang out with him and others, talking soccer. In his magic van, German had albums of photos in which people who had played with him were recorded. I could recognize some of the guys when they were much younger. One of them, whom everyone called Brazil, told me he had been playing with German for more than twenty years. German had been the one organizing games from the beginning, although he'd had some drug and booze problems and had taken a few years off at one point. But he came back, Brazil said. I understood, for the first time since my arrival, that it was possible to live in this country and still have a past shared with other people.

It wasn't clear to me why German was doing it all. Even though I like to think of myself as a reasonably generous person, I could never imagine spending every single weekend putting together soccer games and refereeing, subjecting myself to verbal and other abuse, dismantling the goals and loading up the van long after everybody had left, then washing a large number of T-shirts stinky with worldly sweat. It was clear that without German those pickup games would not be happening, but he never asked for anything in return from us.

I abused for years German's inexplicable generosity. As we often played in the winter in a church gym in Pilsen, which was beyond the reach of my bike, I'd catch a ride in his clunky "Kick me make my day" van, holding the passenger-side door, whose lock didn't work. On the way back, I often feared for my life, as German was prone to celebrating the successful completion of yet another game with a few beers—he always had a well-stocked cooler in his van. He'd talk incessantly, driving and sipping beer, telling me about his favorite team of all time (the Cameroon of the 1990 World Cup) or about his search for an heir, someone who'd continue organizing the games once he retired and moved to Florida. He had a hard time finding the right person, he said, because few people had the guts to commit. He never suggested that I take over, which slightly offended me even if I knew that, gutless as I was, I'd never be able to do it.

Once, during a bloodcurdling ride home on the icy streets of Chicago, I asked him why he was doing it all. He was doing it for God, he said. God had instructed him to put people together, to spread His love, and that became his mission. I was uncomfortable, afraid that he might proselytize, so I didn't ask him anything beyond that. But he never asked people about their religion, never flaunted his faith, never tried to call them to the Lord; his faith in soccer was unconditional; people's belief in the game was enough for him. He told me that, after his retirement, he was planning to buy a piece of land in Florida and build a church, and put a soccer field next to it. He was planning to spend the rest of his life preaching. After the sermons, his flock would play and he would referee.

A few years after that conversation, at the end of the summer, German retired. One of the last weekends before he stopped showing up by the lake, we were playing in sweltering heat. Everybody was testy; hummingbird-size flies were ravenous; the field was hard, humidity high, humility low; a few scuffles broke out. The sky was darkening over the line of skyscrapers along Lake Shore Drive, rain simmering in the clouds, about to boil over. And then a cold front hit us, as if somebody had opened a gigantic cooler, and rain arrived abruptly. I'd never seen anything like that: the rain started at the other end of the field and then moved across it toward the far goal, steadily advancing, like a German World Cup team. We bolted away from the rain, but it quickly caught up with us and in no time we were soaked. There was something terrifying about the blind power of the sudden weather shift, about its violent randomness—as rain washed in waves over us, nothing depended on our minds or wills.

I ran toward German's van, as toward an ark, escaping the flood. There were other guys there already: German; Max from Belize; a man from Chile (consequently known as Chile); Rodrigo, German's mechanic, who miraculously kept the van alive for more than twenty years; and Rodrigo's droopy, bare-chested buddy, who didn't seem to speak English at all, sitting on the cooler, occasionally handing out beers. We took shelter in the van; the rain clattered against the roof, as though we were in a coffin, somebody dropping shovelfuls of dirt on us.

So I asked German if he thought he'd be able to find people to play with in Florida. He was sure he'd find somebody, he said, for if you gave and asked for nothing in return, someone was bound to take. Suddenly inspired, Chile rambled off something that seemed to be a badly learned lesson from a New Age manual, something vapid about unconditional surrender. People in Florida are too old and they can't run, I said. If they're old, German said, they are close to entering eternity, and what they need is hope and courage. Soccer would help them on the way to eternal life, he said.

Now, I'm an atheist man, vain and cautious. I give little, expect a lot, and ask for more—what he was saying seemed far too heavy, naïve, and simplistic. It would have, in fact, seemed heavy, naïve, and simplistic if the following was not taking place:

Hakeem, the Nigerian who somehow found a way to

play soccer every day of his life, runs up, soaked, to the van and asks us if we've seen his keys. Are you out of your mind, we say, as the rain is pouring through the window. Can't you see it's the end of the fucking world, look for your keys later. *Kids*, he says, I'm looking for my *kids*. Then we watch Hakeem running through the rain, collecting his two terrified kids hiding under a tree. He moves like a shadow against the intensely gray curtain of rain, the kids hanging on his chest like little koalas. Meanwhile, on the bike path, Lalas (nicknamed after the American soccer player) stands beside his wife, who is in a wheelchair. She has a horrific case of fast-advancing MS and cannot move fast enough to get out of the rain. They stand together, waiting for the calamity to end: Lalas in his Uptown United T-shirt, his wife under a piece of cardboard slowly and irreversibly dissolving in the rain. The Tibetan goalie and his Tibetan friends, whom I'd never seen before and never would after that day, are playing a game on the field, which is now completely covered with water, as if running in slow motion on the surface of a placid river. The ground is giving off vapor, the mist touching their ankles, and at moments it seems that they're levitating above the flood. Lalas and his wife are perfectly calm watching them, as if nothing could ever harm them. (She has passed away since that day, somebody rest her soul.) They see one of the Tibetans scoring a goal, the rain-heavy ball sliding between the hands of the goalie, who lands in a puddle. He is untroubled, smiling, and from where I sit, he could well be the Dalai Lama himself.

So this, ladies and gentlemen, is what this little narrative is about: the rare moment of transcendence that might be familiar to those who play sports with other people; the moment, arising from the chaos of the game, when all your teammates occupy an ideal position on the field; the moment when the universe seems to be arranged by a meaningful will that is not yours; the moment that perishes—as moments tend to—when you complete a pass. And all you are left with is a vague, physical, orgasmic memory of the evanescent instant when you were completely connected with everything and everyone around you.

THE PATINA

After German left for Florida, I played in a park at Belmont, south of Uptown. It was a wholly different crowd: a lot more Europeans, thoroughly assimilated Latinos, and a few Americans. Often, when I got too excited and demanded, shall we say, that other players stay in their position and play for the team, someone would tell me, Relax, it's just exercise . . . , whereupon I'd suggest that if they couldn't play the way the game's supposed to be played, they should fuck themselves and go and run on a fucking treadmill. No Uptown player would've ever said a thing like that. Relaxation never played any part in our game.

One of the Belmont people was Lido, a seventy-five-year-old Italian. Even the slowest ball was capable of outrunning him, so when the teams were picked he was never counted as a player—we just tolerated his being on the pitch, safe in the assumption that he would have little impact. Like many a man over fifty, Lido was totally delusional about his physical prowess. He truly believed he was still as great a player as he might've been some fifty years ago. Topped with a lamentable toupee he never failed to wear, which would turn to cover his eyes if he headed the ball, he was prone to discussing, after he lost the ball, all his brilliant intentions and all your obvious errors. Lido was a good, decent man. (He passed away in 2011, somebody rest his soul.)

I'd retained the habit of showing up early for games, forever tormented by the possibility of not being allowed to join in. Lido lived nearby and was often there before everyone else. Now and then, he'd arrive flustered and annoyed because he'd seen one of our American fellow players hiding in the park, careful to stay away from us in order to avoid the pregame chitchat. What kind of people are they? Lido grumbled. What are they afraid of? Such a thing would never happen in Italy, he said. Lido was originally from Florence and proudly wore a purple Fiorentina jersey. In Italy, he said, people are always happy to talk to you and help you. If you're lost and ask them for directions, they're willing to leave their stores and houses unattended to take you where you need to go. And they talk to you nicely, politely, and not like *these*—and he flung his hand dismissively toward the trees and bushes behind which the shy Americans were cowering. When I asked him how often he went to Italy, he said he didn't go too often. In Florence, he kept a beautiful Ferrari, he explained, and there were a lot of jealous people there: they would steal his wheels, smash his blinkers, scratch the doors with a nail, for no reason other than sheer malice. He didn't like to go, he said, because people in Italy are not very nice. When I cautiously reminded him that just a few sentences ago Italians had been incredibly nice, he nodded and exclaimed, Yes, yes, very nice! and I gave up. It seemed that Lido was able to hold in his head two mutually exclusive thoughts without inner conflict—a quality, I realized in a flash, not uncommon among artists.

Lido had come to Chicago in the fifties. In Florence, he and his brother had a business restoring Renaissance frescoes and old paintings, apparently a dime a dozen over there. After they'd arrived in America, they figured there were a lot of paintings in need of restoration over here and they started a business. He'd been doing pretty well since, which allowed him to enjoy life to its full extent. He'd been spotted with a young, endowed beauty or two clinging to his forearms or enjoying a ride in his American Ferrari. Besides the beauties, he seemed to have had several wives. The most recent wife was eighteen or so and was, rumor had it, a mail-order bride who came from a small town in Mexico.

Once, while waiting for the Americans to overcome their shyness, Lido explained to me how dilettantes and buffoons had ruined, under the pretense of restoring it, the ceiling of the Sistine Chapel, Michelangelo's masterpiece. Despite my rich ignorance on the matter, he outlined for me all the errors they had committed—they had, for example, used solvent and sponges to take the patina off the frescoes. Lido insisted that I imagine *that*, and I did: I obediently imagined sponging the helpless Michelangelo. Lido got all worked up and, at that moment, cleaning up the Michelangelo with sponges and solvent verily appeared to me as a grievous act—I pictured a God far too pale to be omnipotent, or even moderately powerful.

But the idiots in charge of the restoration, Lido went on, did eventually realize they had screwed up the creation of the Universe according to Michelangelo and they begged Lido to come over to fix it. Instead of coming to their aid, Lido sent them a five-page invective, in essence suggesting that they shove the sponges and solvent up their asses. What they didn't understand, Lido said, was that the patina is the essential part of the fresco, that the world the Almighty created on the ceiling of the Sistine Chapel was *incomplete* until the mortar fully absorbed the paint, until the inchoate universe turned a little darker. It wasn't a sunny day when God created the world, Lido thundered; devoid of the patina it was all worth shit.

As he told me this, Lido was sitting on his ball (size 4, overinflated) and, in his righteous ire, he made the wrong move and slid off it, tumbling onto the ground. I helped him get up, feeling the wrinkled, worn-out skin on his elbow, touching his human patina.

Then the sheepish Americans finally emerged out of the bushes and trees, the rest of the soccer players arrived, and

Lido—the man who took any disrespect toward Michelangelo and the Creation as a personal insult—installed himself in the attack, ready as ever to score a spectacular goal.

Whoever created Lido ought to be satisfied: Lido was one of those rare humans who achieved completion. The rest of us had no choice but to roll in the dirt, get weatherbeaten, and accumulate a patina, hoping to earn our right to simply, unconditionally *be*. And when I passed the ball to Lido that day—fully aware that it was going to be miskicked and wasted—I had the pleasant, tingling sensation of being connected with something bigger and better than me, a sensation wholly inaccessible to those who think soccer is about exercise and relaxation.

THE LIVES OF GRANDMASTERS

■ ■ ■

I

I do not know how old I was when I learned to play chess. I could not have been older than eight, because I still have a chessboard on whose side my father inscribed, with a soldering iron, "Saša Hemon 1972." I loved the board more than chess—it was one of the first things I owned. Its materiality was enchanting to me: the smell of burnt wood that lingered long after my father had branded it; the rattle of the thickly varnished pieces inside, the smacking sound they made when I put them down, the board's hollow wooden echo. I can even recall the taste—the queen's tip was pleasantly suckable; the pawns' round heads, not unlike nipples, were sweet. The board is still at our place in Sarajevo, and, even if I haven't played a game on it in decades, it is still my most cherished possession, providing incontrovertible evidence that there once lived a boy who used to be me.

The branded board was the one Father and I always played on. It would be my job to set up the pieces, after he offered me the choice of one of his fists, enclosing a black or a white pawn. More often than not, I'd choose the hand with the black piece, whereupon Father would dismiss my attempt to negotiate. We'd play and I'd lose, each and every time. My mother objected to his never letting me win, as she believed that children needed to experience the joy of victory to succeed. Father, on the other hand, was ruthlessly firm in his conviction that everything in life had to be earned and that wanting victory always helped achieve it. As an engineer who had faith in unsentimental reasoning, he believed in the hard benefits of knowledge acquired by trying and failing—even if, as in my case, it was exclusively failing.

I would not have admitted it then, but I did crave his furtive encouragement; that is, I wanted Father to let me win, but I didn't want to know that. I was not capable of thinking more than one or two moves in advance (my preferred activities were always soccer and skiing, where you make decisions by improvising inside a vanishing moment). I regularly blundered, leaving my king hopelessly isolated or not spotting the imminent execution of the queen. I reliably fell into all of my father's traps and was much too quick to resign so as to spare myself further humiliation. But more of it was inevitable, as Father would force me to retrace all of the missteps leading to my demise. He prodded me to think about chess in a focused manner—and, by extension, to think thoroughly about everything else: life, physics, family, homework. He gave me a chess textbook (by, of all people, Isidora's father) and, move by move, we analyzed the games played by the great grandmasters such as Lasker, Capablanca, Alekhine, Tal, Spassky, Fischer, et cetera. Patient though Father was with me, I could seldom see all the glorious possibilities of a wise opening or a clever sacrifice. He was trying to take me to a far-too-distant horizon, with all the mysterious comforts of chess architecture, as far as I was concerned, deferred into a dubious future. Going over the grandmasterly games felt too much like school—occasionally interesting, often straining my mind in unpleasant ways. Even so, when alone, I'd try to study chess, hoping that I could glean a simple trick or two before the next game and catch my father by surprise. Instead, I constantly and quickly hit the low ceiling of my abstract-thinking abilities. It didn't help that grandmasters such as Capablanca, Alekhine, and Fischer appeared to be obsessive hermits; I was not a writer yet and could not appreciate the devout artist producing painfully inapplicable art. And the world around me was nothing if not an infinity of distractions: cute girls, novels and comic books, my budding record collection, neighborhood boys whistling from the playground under my window, beckoning me to a soccer game.

Compared with the other kids my age, however, I was not all that bad at chess. The games I played with my friends mainly consisted of blunders and oversights, but I often won them. We played chess the way we played all the other childhood games: heedlessly pursuing the rush of an arbitrary victory, already invested in the next thing to do. I much preferred winning to thinking and I didn't like losing at all. I'd managed to acquire a repertoire of standard openings and attack strategies and was thus capable of committing fewer blunders and outlasting my opponents. I sought opponents who eagerly fell into my textbook traps and subsequently submitted themselves to wholesale destruction. Trash-talking had far more value to me than the highfalutin beauty of brilliant combinations.

When I was in fourth grade, a teacher was assigned to organize an in-school tournament in order to assemble a chess team for an intraschool competition. I signed up. I wanted to challenge myself and go it all alone, but I foolishly told my father about it, so that when I went to play, one Saturday morning, he insisted on accompanying me. He coerced the teacher, who really did not care that much about chess, into letting him rearrange the desks, set up the boards, and design the score chart. Not only was he much too involved, he was the *only* parent involved. In the fourth-grade classroom, furnished with the little desks and chairs, he stood out like a giant. Everyone knew whose father he was.

It is highly possible that I would've done better in that tournament had my father's chess shadow not loomed over me as he watched at my shoulder. I kept staring at the board, envisioning all the errors and possibilities from his point of view, but I saw nothing. One's good fortune is often in the failings of others, so I managed to win some games. It is likely that my father simply distracted the other kids more than me, intimidating them with his silent, coaching presence.

Whatever might have happened, I made it onto the chess team, and a couple of weeks later we took a bus to play against a blind children's team at their school in Nedžarići—a neighborhood so far off for me at that time it was practically a different city. I went as the fifth of eight boards, but it turned out that only four boards were needed, so I spent the day loitering in the depressing hallways of the ramshackle school for the blind and occasionally witnessing the blind kids tearing my teammates to humbled shreds. I had passionately wanted to play, but, watching the slaughter, I was glad to be spared. The blind kids frowned and shook their heads over the boards, clutching pieces with spikes on the underside, then palpating the squares for the holes to fit them in.

I tried to picture a mental space within which the game existed for them, an interiority where all the combinations, all the lines of advance and defensive positions, were—evidently—sharply outlined. But what I saw instead— and what, I thought, they had no way of seeing—was the banal solidity of nonnegotiable physical reality, the ineluctable modality of the visible, past which I could see nothing. A ten-year-old boy, I happily operated in exteriority, retreating inside only when I was reading. The world in all its hackneyed, stubborn concreteness could never be fully suspended for me so that I could think inside the abstract space of the game. When I played with my father, for instance, his very corporeal presence was a terrible distraction. I could never separate the game from our relationship and everything surrounding it: his knee jumped at a rapid speed, jerked by his compulsive foot; his big hands with flat, wide thumbs moved the pieces with defeating confidence; he nodded as he discovered opportunities fully invisible to me; the smell of food floated from the kitchen; my mother lingered on the horizon, imploring my father, yet again, not to checkmate me. Whereupon he would checkmate me.

Naturally, I reached the point of always declining his invitation to play—I claimed I was still training, learning, getting ready. But when he played against čika-Žarko, his college friend, I'd kibitz and listen to their trash-talking. Somewhat guiltily, I'd root against my father. I wanted to witness his defeat, so that he could understand how I might have felt when we played. While he wanted to teach me what he knew, I wanted him to see what it all looked like for me— perhaps love is a process of finding a common vision of reality. I wanted us to share the sense that the number of wrong moves far exceeds the number of good moves, to share the frightening instability of the correct decision, to bond in being confounded. These days, of course, I remember neither his defeats nor his victories; nor do I remember enjoying his being humbled. On the screen of my memory, he is perpetually pouting over the pieces, jerking his foot at a speed commensurate with his difficult position on the board. He loves being inside himself, I imagine; he loves solving problems in the laboratory of his engineering mind; he loves the space in which reason and logic rule. He loves me.

2

In high school, I was in an advanced class. My classmates and I had about twelve hours a week of math and physics, all at the expense of the humanities and natural sciences. We pored over differential calculus and imaginary numbers, struggled with quantum physics and complex functions, while our equivalents in "normal" classes, who had a hard time grasping basic fractions, roamed the sunny, fertile fields of art, music, and biology, learning what all high school kids are good at learning—nothing in particular.

I'd decided to enroll in the math-major class because I'd developed a fascination with the theory of relativity. Having read a number of popular-science articles on Einstein's theory and its flabbergasting implications (space-time! black holes! dark matter!), I'd concluded that the work of a theoretical physicist consisted of staring at the stars and imagining alternative universes, which seemed to me like something I could do for a living. But soon after I'd started high school I was forced to recognize that all I could hope for in the domain of mathematical thinking was to wing it, and from thereon in I was winging it.

My class was a geek-rich environment, with a tragically

low number of young ladies interested in random snuggling. Other classes had a lot more women, all of whom were beyond our reach, permanently repelled by the dark matter of nerdiness we were emitting. Soon we were known in our high school by a derogatory name: the grocers, as calculating grocery expenses seemed to be the only application of math other high school kids could imagine.

There were quite a few considerably talented mathematicians in my class and at least one certifiable genius. His name was Mladen and he was decidedly uncool—he wore V-neck sweaters and pants with an ironed crease; his hair was blown and parted into a pompadour; he paid attention in class, did not curse or speak in slang, had no interest in rock 'n' roll or soccer, and was an unabashedly nice guy, forgoing all the adolescent male posturing. The math problems we grappled with were baby food to him; he lived comfortably inside the bright and arid space of mathematics. Once, as we were jogging in circles next to each other in our PE class, he told me, out of the blue, "Your trajectory is longer than mine," and I had no idea what he was talking about until he explained that, because he was on the inside, my circles were wider than his. Before the end of our freshman year, he won a gold medal at the International Mathematical Olympiad in Washington, D.C., while my accomplishments included reading *The Catcher in the Rye*, becoming a smoker, and transitioning from Led Zeppelin to XTC, as well as resigning myself to academic mediocrity.

Given that we had no access to high school girls and their bodies, we played a lot of chess. Often we organized entire tournaments. We played during class time, while our teachers were completely oblivious to it all. The score chart was pasted to the classroom wall, Mladen always at the top of it, head and shoulders better than any of us. He was so good, in fact, that he could play blindfold games on multiple boards, sometimes against as many as six, all the while paying close attention to the teacher and studiously copying from the chalkboard. We would risk reprimand, hiding our chessboards under our desks, fully ignoring the learning going on. Upon analyzing the position at hand, each of us would send him a note, reading, for example, "Ke2 to e4." Without losing the thread of the teacher's explanation, he would quickly respond with a move. We could instantly see the brilliance of his thinking and recognize we were being demolished. In revenge, we would mock the way in which he wiped the chalkboard clean, sticking his butt out while pulling down the sponge in straight, parallel lines.

The only one who could even begin to compete with Mladen was Ljubo. I'd known him in elementary school. Back then, when I'd pretended to be the George in a Beatles cover band, he'd taken a crack at being the Ringo. By high school, however, Ljubo lost interest in rock 'n' roll and indeed in most things outside the realm of mathematics and chess. Unlike the neat, disciplined, well-groomed Mladen, Ljubo was relentlessly sloppy, fully compliant with the stereotype of an absentminded mathematician. His handwriting was so illegible that he sometimes received low grades in math tests simply because the teacher could not decode his brilliant solutions to difficult equations. Contaminated by the neoromantic myths of unconventionality (Bukowski! Sex Pistols! Warhol!), I thought that his inability to function within the reality everyone else was confined by was a mark of true genius—he, I thought, could end up being the great one among us.

In our junior year, Mladen decided that he was done playing blindfold games with patzers and explaining complex-function graphs to buffoons like me. Within a few months, he passed all the necessary exams, graduated from high school, enrolled in college, and disappeared into the netherland of responsible life. The rest of the grocer patzers had to jump through the hoops of baccalaureate exams before graduation, only to serve in the military for a mandatory year of conscription.

Ljubo, who was too slovenly and disorganized to do what Mladen did and thus avoid serving in the army, had a dreadful time as a conscript. He came back from the army terribly distraught, in spite of which he passed all the difficult math exams in his first year of college. The only exam he had problems with was in geometry, because he had to draw graphs and keep them neat. He would come to the exam unshaven and bepimpled, his unwashed shirt untucked, a broken ruler and a single blunt pencil in hand. The graphs he had to draw for the exam seemed to represent his complexly muddled mind far more than simple euclidean space.

Soon he was enmeshed in full-fledged schizophrenia. A couple of times he was locked up in Jagomir, a grim funhouse close to the city zoo on the outskirts of Sarajevo. I never went to visit him there, but a few of my classmates did. They came back with dreadful stories of small rooms packed with patients serving imaginary coffee in imaginary pots to imaginary guests or huddling in the corners and howling in unreal pain. For his visitors, Ljubo unfurled long and elaborate tales of intricate conspiracies, scoffing at his classmates for failing to see the obvious connections between remote possibilities. Unlike Ljubo, they had no voices to guide them through his chaotic interiority and they listened to him, helplessly, bemused.

Once, after Ljubo returned to his parents' home from Jagomir, his mother called us up and suggested that we come over to talk to him and cheer him up. The seven of us, his high school friends, rang the bell sheepishly, giggling with discomfort, and offered our chocolate-bonbon presents to his distressed mother. She served us soft drinks and snacks, as if we were at a birthday party, and then left us alone, no doubt to press her ear against the door. We babbled awkwardly, because Ljubo was not well at all and we didn't know what to say. He was listless and slow, affected by strong antipsychotic medication. Then we listened in stunned silence as he spun his schizo-narratives. This time, he divulged to us the true story of Alekhine, who, in Ljubo's rendition, descended directly from God himself and therefore partook in some sort of destiny-control mechanism, plainly visible to those who analyzed his games correctly. Somehow, Alekhine's divinity had been transferred to Ljubo, who was thus in direct communication with God. We had no idea, he told us, about the things that were happening as we spoke, we had no way to grasp the magnitude of his still-unused powers. The Alekhine yarn was then threaded into his claim that the truly great grandmasters—those of Alekhine's divine caliber—all eventually quit playing the game. Because the number of various positions in chess, however immense, was finite, the true grandmasters eventually played their way through all the possible combinations, thereby reaching the outer limits of chess. At that point, they got bored, as there were no more games they could play. We listened to him, rapt. He continued: once the great grandmasters were done with chess, they'd switch to inverse chess, where the goal was to lose quickly—whoever lost first, won the game. This game of inverse chess was called *bujrum*, which in Bosnian means something like "serve yourself" and is used to offer food at the table. Thus you offered your pieces to the other player, trying to lose as many as possible as soon as possible and then put yourself in a checkmate position. I'd played *bujrum* as a kid, oblivious to the possibility of treading upon divine turf. All the greatest grandmasters, Ljubo said, were now playing *bujrum*, Bobby Fischer included. Many of the greatest *bujrum* players were unheard-of. Karpov and Kasparov (furiously involved at the time in a rivalry over the world champion title) were actually just pathetic patzers, not able to cross the *bujrum* border to the other side of chess.

His troubled conviction was so strong that the story made sense for a moment—we had to snap out of it to dismiss it, still saying nothing. We knew no way of responding to his ramblings, nor could we come up with a counterargument that could even begin to weaken his psychotic faith. We sat brooding, until his mother came in with more pretzels and Coke. We quickly went for the snacks, grasping at the junk food straws, stuffing our mouths to avoid saying anything. We were hoping that we could be released now, but Ljubo's mother wanted to keep the party going, so she suggested to Ljubo that he play something on the accordion for us. Acquiescently, he fetched his instrument. We waited as he adjusted the straps at a glacial speed. We recognized the first bars of the "Ode to Joy"; none of us expected him to play Beethoven on his discordant accordion. Slowly stretching and squeezing it, he produced notes and wheezes perfectly devoid of any semblance of joy. To this day, Ljubo's interpretation of the last movement of Beethoven's Ninth is the saddest piece of music—indeed the saddest humanly generated sound—I have ever heard. What he played for us was to music what *bujrum* was to chess: his rendition was absolutely the opposite of the "Ode to Joy." We were paralyzed by the frightening possibilities implied by his antimusic and antichess. Beyond our life there was antilife and he was living it; we had not known it, until we heard the anti–"Ode to Joy." We idiotically applauded, guzzled down our fizzless Coke, thanked his mother, and went home to try to live without the fear of antimatter and darkness.

3

In the early nineties, after I'd moved from Ukrainian Village to Edgewater, I played chess at a place in Rogers Park called the Atomic Cafe. It was a few blocks away from the Artists in Residence building, where I was renting a tiny studio. The café was next door to the 400 Movie Theater, where one could watch second-run movies for a couple of bucks and which reeked of stale popcorn and permanently clogged toilet. In the summer, people played chess in a fenced-off outdoor seating area; the rest of the year, the café was full of students from nearby Loyola University, with a corner always occupied by chess enthusiasts. North Side players convened every day to play at the café; on weekends, one could easily play for twelve hours straight. The first time I wandered in, sometime in the early summer of 1993, I kibitzed for a while before going off for a movie. The following day, I returned to the café hoping to play a game. After sheepishly watching, I summoned enough confidence to accept a challenge by an older man who introduced himself as Peter. He looked shabby: gray hair peeking in tufts out of his ears, a flannel shirt on the verge of snapping open at his potbelly, envelopes sticking halfway out of his chest pocket. For some reason, he exuded a strong smell of perfume. But he appeared very wise to me as he narrowed his brows to examine the position on the board. Much like one can tell a good soccer player from the way he or she touches the ball with his or her foot, I could tell Peter was serious about chess from the way he sank deep into himself to contemplate the next move and all the possibilities beyond it.

I don't remember how the first game against Peter went down, but I'm confident I lost it—it had been a while since I'd played a demanding game. But I kept going back to the café, playing more and more, often with Peter, who never seemed to get bored with beating me. I played with others, too, and even began winning against some respectable regulars. Pretty soon, I was spending weekends at the café, breaking up the long chess hours only to see a movie next door.

It turned out the Atomic Cafe was rife with all kinds of characters obsessed with chess. Between the games I would hang out with the idle players, small-talking, asking them a lot of questions, ever eager to extract bits of other people's lives. There was a Vietnam vet, for instance, who had been on disability at least since the fall of Saigon. His knee often jerked rapidly and he was proud of having helped stop the advance of communism in Southeast Asia. He played chess, took drugs, and did little else. Once, he described to me putting his face, high on acid, under a stream of water to examine the oncoming water drops—their molecular beauty fucking blew his fucking mind. There was Marvin the Master, the size and shape of a football player, who would occasionally stop by the café to play speed-chess games, disposing of the patzers at such speed and with such brilliance that no one in the admiring crowd could see what was happening. There was a brilliant Indian computer programmer who, in the few years I frequented the place, lost a number of jobs because of his chess obsession. He promised his wife at least once he would quit, but he could not help thinking of chess incessantly. Failing to stay clean of chess, he still came to the café, but declined all invitations to play, wasting just as much time kibitzing. Predictably, he ended up getting divorced. He told me so himself, the last time I saw him. He was driving a cab at the time, which he parked in front of the café to play all day, happily off the wagon and thoroughly uninterested in catching fares. All my chess friends seemed to be lonely men, continuously struggling to reproduce the painfully evanescent beauty of the game, never getting within sight of the *bujrum* border.

Then there was Peter. Playing against him, I would attack from all sides, and he would patiently defend, waiting for me to make a mistake. Inescapably, I would make one, and he would enter the endgame with an extra pawn, inexorably advancing toward becoming a queen. Soon I would be forced to acknowledge defeat, whereupon he would jokingly demand my resignation in writing. We didn't talk much while playing, but would chitchat between games, exchanging basic information and finding things in common. He lived in and owned a perfume shop in the neighborhood, which explained his rich, ever-changing flowery scent, heretofore incongruous with his shabby-old-man appearance. We both came from elsewhere: I told him I was born and raised in Sarajevo, Bosnia, to which he said: "I'm sorry." He, on the other hand, was Assyrian, but born in Belgrade. Walking home after a long day of playing, I asked him how come he'd been born in Belgrade. After a groan of reluctance, in a subdued voice of discomfort, he told me that his parents had escaped from Turkey in 1917 or so, at the time when the Turks had been busy exterminating Armenians, but could still spare, while they were at it, some time and bullets to get rid of a few Assyrians. His parents ended up in Belgrade, so he was born there. A few years later, following a properly unpredictable refugee trajectory, they found themselves in Iraq around the time it became independent, and that was where he'd grown up. But then, in his twenties, he had to leave Iraq because he had a run-in with the prime minister's son (he offered no details or explanation); his life was at risk, so he fled to Iran. He got married, had a son, and, in 1979, was living in Tehran, employed at the American embassy, arguably the worst imaginable place of employment in the case of a local Islamic revolution. During the chaotic upheaval, his only son, conspicuously clad in denim, was stopped and searched on the street by the revolutionaries. He had some pot and they shot him on the spot.

So here was an Assyrian named Peter, selling knock-off Eternity for Men in Chicago, beating me at chess without any particular pleasure; here was a man whose life contained more suffering than I could begin to imagine. The story of

Peter's life was narrated to me along the few blocks we walked before we parted, in five minutes or less. There is always a story, I learned on that walk, more heartbreaking and compelling than yours. And I understood why I was so drawn to Peter: we belonged to the same displaced tribe. I picked him out of the crowd because I recognized the kinship.

I remembered how, a few weeks before, he had gone off at a couple of Loyola students who were babbling at the next table, copiously abusing the word *like*, barely slowing down to take a breath. I'd been annoyed by the incessant vacuousness of their exchange, the idiotic frequency of the *like*s, and I couldn't stop listening precisely because I'd had no idea what they were talking about. But I just put up with it, always liable to distraction. Peter, however, suddenly exploded: "Why are you talking so much?" he yelled at them. "You've been talking for an hour, saying nothing. Shut up! Shut up!" The students shut up, terrified. Peter's outburst, shocking though it may have been, made perfect sense to me—not only did he deplore the waste of words, he detested the moral lassitude with which they were wasted. To him, in whose throat the bone of displacement was forever stuck, it was wrong to talk about nothing when there was a perpetual shortage of words for all the horrible things that happened in the world. It was better to be silent than to say what didn't matter. One had to protect from the onslaught of wasted words the silent place deep inside oneself, where all the pieces could be arranged in a logical manner, where the opponents abided by the rules, where even if you ran out of possibilities there might be a way to turn defeat into victory. The students, of course, could not begin to comprehend the painful infinity of Peter's interior space. Inoculated against speechlessness, they had no access to the unspeakable. They could not see us, even though we were there, as we were nowhere and everywhere. So they shut up and sat in wordless oblivion; then they got up and left. Peter and I arranged the pieces for another game of chess.

4

After a couple of years of regular playing at the Atomic Cafe, I became pretty good for a patzer. To go beyond that, to have a crack at being a truly good player, I would've had to go back to analyzing the great games. That was not going to happen: not only was I too old and lazy, I had no time for studying chess either, as I had to earn the money to feed and clothe the body that sheathed the inner space. Moreover, after a few years of feeling stuck between my mother tongue and my DP language and being incapable of writing in either of them, I finally began writing in English. In doing so, I delimited a new space, where I could process experience and generate stories. Writing was another way to organize my interiority so that I could retreat into it and populate it with words. My need for chess was dissipating, as it was being fulfilled by writing.

Now it seems to me that the last game I ever played was against my father, though that is almost certainly not true—it was just the last one that mattered. I was visiting my parents in Hamilton, Ontario, sometime in 1995, and I challenged Father to a game. Having settled in Canada, my parents were at the nadir of their refugee trajectory, and, it seemed at that time, at the end of their rope. Tormented by the brutal Canadian climate, uncomfortable in the language they were forced to live in, short on friends and family, they were prone to devastating nostalgia and hopelessness.

I was not capable of helping them in any way. During my visits, we argued much too often: their despair annoyed me, because it exactly matched mine and prevented them from offering comfort to *me*—I suppose I still wanted to be their child. We argued over the smallest things, hurtfully remembering and bringing up unresolved fights and unforgotten insults from before the war, only to make up a few minutes later. We missed each other, even while we were together, because the decaying elephant in the room was the loss of our previous life—absolutely nothing was the way it used to be. Everything we did together in Canada reminded us of what we used to do together in Bosnia. Hence we didn't like doing any of it, but had nothing else to do. I spent entire days on the parental sofa (donated by a kind Canadian), watching reruns of *Law and Order*. I would snap out of my TV coma with the urge to scream at somebody, akin to what had driven Peter to terrify the hapless Loyola students.

One of those hopeless days, I challenged my father to a

game. I admit I was burning to beat him; having gone through the Atomic Cafe boot camp, I was ready to discard his shadow after a few decades of not playing against him. I could now redress the long-lasting imbalance between us by winning and putting him in a position to feel what I felt as a boy. I offered him my fists, each clenched around a pawn, to choose; he picked the black one. We set up the pieces on a tiny magnetic board; we played; I won; I found no pleasure in it. Neither did he. It is possible that he finally let me win. If he did, I didn't notice it. We shook hands in silence, like true grandmasters, and never again played against each other.

KENNEL LIFE

∎ ∎ ∎

Sometime in 1995, in the teachers' room of a vocational school where I was teaching English as a Second Language, I met L. In the course of our small-talking she declared that Robert Bresson was her favorite film director. There was a Bresson retrospective at Facets that week and I suggested that we go to see *Pickpocket* together; she consented. On her way to the classroom to teach, she made a little leap getting around a chair and a thought—if that is the word—appeared in my head: I am going to marry that woman. It was not a decision nor a plan; it was unrelated to desire or a sense of connection. It was simply a recognition of an inescapable future: I recognized that I would marry her, the way I recognized it was night at night.

We went to see *Pickpocket*, then, later, *Lancelot du Lac*, which relates the story of Lancelot and Guinevere while stripping it of any romantic fluff—when the knights walk around in their armor you can hear it relentlessly creaking and you imagine the flesh inside it, the rotting sores and all. Afterward, we went for a drink at the Green Mill and I kissed her at the bar; she stood up from the stool and left. She had a boyfriend at the time, and she tracked him down at a party where he was jumping up and down to some exhilarating song; she brought him down to the ground and broke up. Thus we started dating. A year and a half later we were living together; two and a half years later I proposed to her, while tying my shoe—practicing, as it were, the cliché of tying the knot. She didn't hear what I said and I had to repeat it. I had no ring on hand, but she accepted.

We did things together. We traveled: Shanghai, Sarajevo, Paris, Stockholm; I taught her to ski; she had grown up in Chicago and told me stories of the city I could not have known otherwise; we lived in a house where the front doorbell rang if you stamped your foot at a particular spot on the kitchen floor; we bought an apartment with two fireplaces; we had a cat and it died. Once, she took the ring off to wash her hands and it fell and rolled across the floor straight into a heating vent, never to be found. We both thought of ourselves as decent people and loved each other enough to cover up the cracks, which started appearing pretty soon.

It took a few years for me to gradually realize we shouldn't have tied the knot, but I'd inherited the concept of marriage from my parents that was contingent upon, like everything else in their lives, hard work. Thus the operating metaphor of our marriage for me was the mine—as in, being married was like descending into a mine every day and digging for some valuable ore. The possibility of a functioning, rewarding marriage was dependent on the grueling effort put into it, which is to say that being simply happy was perpetually deferred into some hypothetical future—if we kept digging we would one day be happy. But there might never have been enough ore for us to dig; and at the end of each daily shift, I was angry and exhausted. Soon, periods of reasonable calm, squeezed between destructive fights, were taken to be the ore of happiness. We reached the point of accepting not-fighting as the goal and purpose of our marital union. We showed and recognized love only in the form of trying hard to make up. What we offered to each other in lieu of deep affection was gestures of either reconciliation or aggression— sometimes, confusingly, both at the same time. I had frequent outbursts of anger, the congealed life-inflicted hurt I did not know how to heal; I flung it around hatefully, like offal.

The end of my first marriage came unexpectedly, even if it was a long time in coming, because the pain and misery were now habitual, a side effect of descending daily into the mine. I kept finding myself angrily building my case against L., ever waiting for an opportunity to lay out the irrefutable evidence that none of it was my fault, that I was in fact the one wronged, the one with more pain inside. It finally ended at the top of the umpteenth screaming match, unremarkable in and of itself. The confrontation had a recognizable, well-practiced pattern that inescapably led to my screaming and smashing objects at hand. It would have been normally followed by a period of horrible guilt on my part for losing control and hurting L. yet again—guilt was all that was left to connect us toward the end. This time, in the middle of it all, a thought—if that is the word—appeared in my head: I could not do this anymore. There was nothing I wanted to say or prove to L.; nothing was worth fighting and nothing was worth trying. My bottom fell out and, as in a Zen parable, I was emptied of all the anger and love in an instant— I ended my mining life in less than a minute. That night in January 2005, I drove L., through a torrent of tears, to her mother's place in Indiana, then drove back to our empty apartment.

Once a marriage ends, what is left is the heavy-footed dance of dissolution. I could not bear staring at the cold fireplaces, and within a week I was looking for temporary, furnished lodgings, where I could stay until the mess was sorted out. My funds were limited, which meant the places I was hurriedly considering were rather dismal. Each of the dreadfully furnished apartments was shown to me by a building manager who despised the people desperate enough to live in such places; each had a door opening directly into the world of thick, gloomy loneliness. One studio available in the fancy Gold Coast neighborhood looked as though someone had just been murdered in it and the management had been considerate enough to whitewash the blood-spattered walls.

After a few days' search, I settled for a studio on the top floor of a three-story building on Chicago's Northwest Side. The landlady—let us grace her with the name Mary—lived on the second floor. She was an adoption lawyer; she showed me pictures of happy, overlit couples, the babies bewildered by their new destiny in their adoptive parents' laps. Mary appeared to me as a generous, embracive woman, the kind that accepted derelicts, canine and human. She didn't ask too many questions and had no interest in my unimpressive credit history, so I gallantly wrote her a check on the spot. Check in hand, she said she hoped I didn't mind dogs, for she kept several and was active at a dog shelter. I loved dogs myself, I confessed, and told her a little bit about Mek; she oohed and aahed. Her place seemed as good as any for my upcoming bouts of self-pity.

I went back to my former home, packed a couple of suitcases, loaded them into my Honda Civic along with my stereo, and rode west into the sunset.

One of the few tapes in my car at the time was *Hank Williams 40 Greatest Hits*, and I listened to it every time I drove. The sense of entering a new life can make almost anything seem significant or prophetic, and I couldn't help imagining myself as a *ramblin' man*—the man old Hank had written the song about—as I drove to Mary's *mansion on the hill*.

The signification haze, however, somehow failed to envelop the overwhelming stench I noticed a couple of days after moving in. I tried to remember whether I'd smelled anything when Mary showed me the studio but I could recall nothing irking my nose. I spent a lot of time parsing the stench, as though understanding it would make it bearable—a common intellectual fallacy. Besides the expectable dog shit and piss, there were other perplexing ingredients: generic miasma, a touch of rank cat litter (for there were, it turned out, a couple of cats as well), fetid coffee, a whiff of weak disinfectant. Most dominant was cheap dog food, somehow tucked inside the smell of Crisco, as though Mary deep-fried it for her puppies.

Ready for any and all new challenges, I thought I could get used to the odor, but it was getting worse by the day. At some point it was so intense that I went to a supermarket on the spur of a particularly stinking moment, determined to splurge on luxurious air fresheners. But slouching toward a divorce made me cheap—I found Air Wicks on sale and I bought enough Green Apple and Honeysuckle to offset the reek of a house full of rotting cadavers. At first, there was nothing but the sugary scent in my studio, but then the two smells merged. I'd never before known anything like the olfactory concoction of the deep-fried dog food and Green Apple and Honeysuckle, and I hope I never will again.

Soon I met the dogs themselves. As I was going down the back stairs to the laundry room, I was intercepted by three proud mutts. Two of them were overweight, with wide hips and dull eyes; the third one was small, skinny, and manic, and quickly recognizable as a humper—indeed he instantly tried to fuck my shin. Mary introduced them to me, and I'm afraid I can remember only the name of the biggest one—he was Kramer. On my way back from the laundry room, they followed me, and the moment I stepped into my studio, before the door was even closed, Kramer pissed at my doorstep.

Almost every time I went down to the laundry room I had to slalom between shit piles and piss puddles, only to encounter the dogs. Occasionally the trio would be reinforced with a new mangy mutt Mary's neighbors had dropped off in her backyard, which appeared to serve as a makeshift dog shelter. New mutts came and went, but Kramer and Skinny Fuck (as I referred to that adorable little creature) and the Third One were a steady lineup.

They, I learned, had distinct, well-defined personalities. Kramer was the decider, Skinny Fuck was a skinny fuck, the Third One was slow and lazy. It was easy to differentiate among them as I lay sleepless in bed and they performed their nightly repertoire of howling and barking. They would start their recital with a choral piece, often set off by a passing bus, but after midnight they usually performed solo, in sequence: the Third One kept me awake for a few hours with a steady, slothful yelp; Skinny Fuck was as enthusiastic about his excitement at two a.m. as he was at any other time; and Kramer covered the early-morning shift, his deep, obdurate voice driving me crazy through the dawn, at which time I was prone to fantasizing about canine crucifixion, one at a time. Once or twice, I spent part of the night remembering Mek and his quiet Irish setter manner—the way his eyes widened when my father whispered something in his ear, or the way he put his head on your thigh, demanding nothing in particular.

Kramer, on the other hand, was my nemesis, the reigning male of the house. He liked to let me know who the big dog was by sniffing me authoritatively every time I walked by, or by defecating disdainfully at my door. Mary mentioned a husband every once in a while, but all the mail was addressed to her and I'd never seen or heard any man on the premises. It was hard to imagine anybody—other than Mary and, with the dubious help of Green Apple and Honeysuckle, me—putting up with the fetid air, but the husband was rhetorically and mysteriously present. I wondered about Mary's missing hubby the day I found the front door of her place wide open, Chief Kramer patrolling the entrance hallway like an Arizona Minuteman. I'd never seen the inside of Mary's apartment. Whenever I'd knocked at her door to deliver the rent check or ask a question, she would open it ajar, because, she would claim, she didn't want to let the dogs out. I was on my way to put in a shift of writing at a fresh-smelling coffee shop, but the open door troubled me. I yelled *Mary!* from the hallway, reluctant to step in lest Kramer tear at my throat, but there was no response. I could see Skinny Fuck stretching and yawning contentedly on top of a laundry pile mounted on the sofa.

Mary! I envisioned Mary's partially devoured body on the kitchen floor. Cautiously, I went in, Kramer close at my heels. To the right, there was a bedroom, and from a pillow on the bed, the dull snout of an unknown mutt stared at me indifferently. All over the apartment, on every surface, including the floor, there was aged, unfolded laundry, ancient newspapers and coupons, food wrappings, and stuff whose shape and purpose were indeterminable. A body could be hidden anywhere in the apartment and safely rot away, the dogs preferring the fresh cadaver to the fried shit notwithstanding. Mary's apartment looked like one of those places that would have to be razed upon the owner's death because it presented a health hazard and could never be cleaned. I ventured deeper into the apartment, closely monitored by the sovereign Kramer, who seemed confident that I could be easily neutralized if I found anything compromising in his domain. A couple of cats sat high up on the kitchen cabinets, glaring at a cage with two birds. The Third One lounged on the floor in the kitchen, where there was a lot more crap— unwashed dishes and Tupperware full of mold, more unfolded laundry and things unknown, the stove buried under a heap of pans, the cat litter I could smell but not see. I was steadily retching by this point. I had discovered the mother lode of the stench, but there were no visible bodies, and I didn't wish to investigate any further. If there were things to be sniffed out, I was going to let the neighbors and the police deal with it. I left Mary's den and went on my way.

Driving to the coffee shop, I slid in the Hank Williams tape, and by typically significant coincidence, the song that started playing was "Move It on Over." I had become fully obsessed with the caninity of my new life. I would refer to my place of lodging as "the kennel"; I would embark upon ecstatic, baffling monologues describing my present dog life to my friends, who often asked why I hadn't moved out—to which I had no answer, and still don't. I might well have suffered from a bad case of disaster euphoria. I would much too frequently use phrases and terms like *dog days*, *dog's life*, *going to the dogs*, *doghouse*; I looked up the whole family of canine-related words: *canicide*, *caniculture*, *caninity*, *canivorous*, et cetera. I even found significance in the fact that there was a great *hot dog* place around the corner from the kennel. It was perfectly natural, then, that I could see myself in "Move It on Over," the song in which Hank comes back home at half past ten to find that his wife has locked him out: "She changed the lock on our front door. / My door key don't fit no more," so he goes to sleep at the doghouse and sings "Move over skinny dog, fat dog's moving in." I'd been a Hank-like man, fully identifiable in these lines: "This doghouse shared is mighty small / But it's better than no house at all."

Projecting yourself until everything is talking about you is, of course, a self-flattering form of self-pity (as though there were any other kind), to which I'd always been prone. I'd been so lonesome I could cry; I'd got the feeling called the blues; I was a rolling stone all alone in love, just another guy on the lost highway—I'd populated many of Hank's songs. But the day I entered Mary's place and faced the nightmare of her life, I had an epiphany: I was a loser, a man who was beginning to convince himself that living out of suitcases and choking on Green Apple and Honeysuckle was freedom.

When I returned later to my doghouse after a lousy day of lousy writing, the door of Mary's apartment was closed. I heard her talking to Kramer and his friends, as they merrily barked. There was a man's voice too, possibly the husband. Upstairs, I clearly saw the negligent lonesomeness that had wreaked havoc upon my life. The filth of my new bachelorhood had accumulated all around the studio: piles of clothes, clusters of food containers, meaningless papers and dog-eared books, gaping suitcases and shaky CD towers; in the kitchen sink, dishes crusted with weeks-old grease; fat flies circled like buzzards over the table that was home now to a nascent ecosystem; in the bathroom, coils of pubic hair in the corners, the toilet bowl sporting a thick grimy collar. I had touched bottom.

The (good) thing is, once you hit bottom the only way is up. It was while living in the kennel that I met Teri. I'd received an e-mail asking me to contribute a piece for what I understood to be a photo book called *Chicago in the Year 2000* and, in late February 2005, I went for a meeting with Teri, who was editing the book. Distracted by the marriage dissolution, I had assumed that Teri was a man, but when a tall, beautiful woman walked out of her office to meet me, I instantly and unquestionably recognized her as *the woman I love*. During our business meeting, I watched how perfectly her face operated; I scanned her office for clues and information about her; I saw a troubling ultrasound picture of a fetus taped to the computer screen, which I thought might have been hers (no, she said, her sister's); I looked at her typing hands, as she was showing me the photos that would go into the book, to see if there was a wedding ring. I agreed to whatever she wanted me to do; I suggested—slyly, I thought—that we discuss it over lunch or dinner.

Before I met Teri, I was going to fill up my newly acquired singlehood with relentless, mindless promiscuity. I was intent on making up the time lost being faithful to L. I reviewed my book tours and literary festival appearances in order to recall all the women who had seemed interested in undertaking a (short) sexual adventure with me. "Remember me? Our eyes locked six years ago and then I looked away," I would say. "But now, with lust in my heart and condoms in my pocket, I am back!" The plan was indefinitely suspended because I fell in love with Teri so fast and so hard that I walked out of her office trying to figure out all that I needed to do to spend the rest of my life with her. The first thing was to invest in some new clothes: as soon as I left her office building, I bought a new, hip jacket, presumably far more suitable for a charming young writer than a retired miner.

We flirted by e-mail; I eagerly explained my postmarital

situation lest I look like a cad; she told me that her grandparents knew Duke Ellington; I sent her a CD of Rosemary Clooney backed by Duke's orchestra. I quickly wrote and submitted the piece for *CITY 2000*, entitled "Reasons Why I Do Not Wish to Leave Chicago: An Incomplete, Random List." One unstated reason was that the city was now marked by Teri's presence in it.

Our first official date was at a Bucktown place called Silver Cloud; we met at midnight, as in a fairy tale. At some point, I went to the bathroom, and as I walked out the Pixies' "Here Comes Your Man" was playing on the sound system. I shamelessly strutted toward Teri in my jacket, offering myself for interpretation and life commitment. She gave me a ride to the kennel; I kissed her. Every living cell in me—and some I'd thought were long dead—wanted to spend a night with her but I knew that, if she smelled the Crisco-fried dog food, if she saw the pubic hair coils in the bathroom, if her delicate foot touched the filthy bottom I had sunk to, I'd never see her again. The following morning, I was going away for a few weeks in Sarajevo and was already missing her, but I did not invite her upstairs.

It was the wisest decision of my life. Within weeks I was living with Teri in her apartment in Ukrainian Village. She had a dog named Wolfie, whom she never, ever let get up on her bed. Within a year we were engaged. Within another we were married.

THE AQUARIUM

■ ■ ■

On July 15, 2010, my wife, Teri, and I took our younger daughter, Isabel, for her regular medical checkup. She was nine months old and appeared to be in perfect health. Her first teeth had come in, and she was now regularly eating with us at the dinner table, babbling and shoveling rice cereal into her mouth by herself. A cheerful, joyous child, she had a fondness of people, which she had not, the joke went, inherited from her congenitally grumpy father.

Teri and I always went together to all the doctor's appointments for our children, and this time we also took along Ella, Isabel's big sister, who was almost three years old. The nurse at Dr. Gonzalzles's office took Isabel's temperature and measured her weight and her height and head circumference, and Ella was happy that she didn't have to undergo the same ordeal. Dr. G—as we called him—listened to Isabel's breathing, checked her eyes and ears. On his computer, he pulled up Isabel's development chart: her height was within the expected range; she was a bit underweight. Everything seemed fine, except for her head circumference, which exceeded two standard measures of deviation. Dr. G was concerned. Reluctant to send Isabel for an MRI, he scheduled an ultrasound exam for the following day.

Back at home, Isabel was restless and cranky; she had a hard time falling and staying asleep. If we hadn't gone to Dr. G's, we would've thought that she was simply tired, but now we had a different interpretative framework, founded on fear. Later that night, I took Isabel out of our bedroom (she always slept with us) to calm her down. In the kitchen, I sang to her my entire lullaby repertoire: "You Are My Sunshine"; "Twinkle, Twinkle, Little Star"; and a Mozart song I'd learned as a child and whose lyrics in Bosnian I miraculously remembered. Singing the three lullabies in a relentless loop usually worked, but this time it took a while before she laid her head on my chest and quieted down. It felt as though she were comforting me, telling me somehow that everything would be all right. Worried as I was, I imagined a future in which I would one day recall that moment and tell someone—Isabel herself, perhaps—how it was she who calmed *me* down. My daughter, I would say, took care of me, and she was but nine months old.

The following morning, Isabel underwent an ultrasound exam of her head, crying in Teri's arms throughout. Shortly after we came back home, Dr. G called and told us the ultrasound showed that Isabel was hydrocephalic and that we needed to go to an emergency room immediately—it was a life-threatening situation.

The ER examination room at Chicago's Children's Memorial Hospital was kept dark, as Isabel was about to have a CT scan and the doctors were hoping she would fall asleep by herself so they wouldn't have to drug her. But she was not allowed to eat, because there was a possibility of a subsequent MRI, and she kept crying with hunger. A resident gave her a colorful whirligig and we blew at it to distract her. In the horrifying dimness of possibilities, we waited for something to come to pass, all too afraid to imagine what it might be.

Dr. Tomita, the head of pediatric neurosurgery, read the CT scans for us: Isabel's ventricles were enlarged, full of fluid. Something was blocking the draining channels, Dr. Tomita said, possibly "a growth." An MRI was urgently needed.

Teri held Isabel in her arms as the anesthetics were administered; her head nearly instantly fell, heavy on Teri's chest. We handed her over to the nurses for an hourlong MRI; this would be the first time we delivered her to complete strangers and walked away to fear the news. The cafeteria in the hospital basement was the saddest place in the world—and forever it shall be—with its grim neon lights and gray tabletops and the diffuse foreboding of those who stepped away from suffering children to have a grilled cheese sandwich. We didn't dare speculate about the results of the MRI; we suspended our imagination, anchored in the moment, which, terrifying as it was, hadn't yet extended into a future.

Called up to medical imaging, we ran into Dr. Tomita in the overlit hallway. "We believe," he said, "that Isabel has a tumor." He showed us the MR images on the computer: right at the center of Isabel's brain, lodged among her cerebellum, brain stem, and hypothalamus, there was a round *thing*. It was the size of a golf ball, Dr. Tomita suggested, but I'd never cared about golf and couldn't envision what he was saying. He would remove the tumor, and we would find out what kind it was only after the pathology report. "But it looks like a teratoid," he said. I couldn't comprehend the word *teratoid* either—it was outside my language and experience, belonging to the domain of the unimaginable and incomprehensible, the domain into which Dr. Tomita was now guiding us.

Isabel was asleep in the recovery room, motionless, innocent; Teri and I kissed her hands and forehead. In twenty-four hours or so, our existence was horribly and irreversibly transformed. At Isabel's bedside, we wept within the moment that was dividing our life into *before* and *after*, whereby the before was forever foreclosed, while the after was spreading out, like an exploding twinkle-star, into a dark universe of pain.

Still unsure of the word Dr. Tomita had uttered, I looked up brain tumors on the Internet and found an image of a tumor nearly identical to the one in Isabel's brain. I recognized the bastard when I saw it, comprehending the word *teratoid* at that moment. The full name was, I read, "atypical teratoid rhabdoid tumor" (ATRT). It was highly malignant and exceedingly rare, a freak occurring in only 3 out of 1,000,000 children, representing about 3 percent of pediatric cancers of the central nervous system. The survival rate for children under three was less than 10 percent. There were more discouraging statistics available for me to ponder, but I recoiled from the screen, deciding instead to talk to and trust Isabel's doctors alone—never again would I research her situation on the Internet. I had a hard time telling Teri about what I had read, because I wanted to protect her from all the horrid possibilities. I understood already that managing knowledge and imagination was necessary for not losing our minds.

On Saturday, July 17, Dr. Tomita and his neurosurgical team implanted an Ommaya reservoir in Isabel's head, so as to help drain and relieve the pressure from her accumulated cerebrospinal fluid (CSF). When she returned to her hospital bed on the neurosurgery floor, Isabel kicked off her blanket, as she had been wont to do; we took it as an encouraging sign, a hopeful first step on a long journey. On Monday, she was released from the hospital to wait at home for the surgery that would remove the tumor, scheduled for the end of the week. We went home to wait.

Teri's parents were in town, because Teri's sister had given birth to her second son on the day of Isabel's checkup—too busy with Isabel's illness, we hardly paid attention to the new arrival in the family—and Ella spent the weekend with her grandparents, barely noticing the upheaval and our related absence. That sunny Tuesday afternoon, we all went out for a walk, Isabel strapped to Teri's chest. The same night, we rushed to the emergency room because Isabel developed a fever, which suggested an infection, not uncommon after the insertion of a foreign object—in this case, the Ommaya—in a child's head.

She received antibiotics for infection and underwent a scan or two; the Ommaya was removed. On Wednesday afternoon, I went back home from the hospital to be with Ella, as we'd promised we would take her to our neighborhood farmer's market—keeping promises was essential in the ongoing catastrophe. We bought blueberries and peaches; on the way home, we picked up some first-rate cannoli from our favorite pastry shop. I talked to Ella about Isabel's being sick, about her tumor, and told her she would have to stay with Grandma that night. She didn't complain or cry, able as well as any three-year-old to understand the difficulty of our predicament.

As I was walking to the car, the cannoli in hand, to get back to the hospital, Teri called and urged me to get there as soon as possible. Isabel's tumor was hemorrhaging; emergency surgery was required. Dr. Tomita was waiting to talk to me before going with Isabel into the operating room. It took me about fifteen minutes to get to the hospital, through traffic that existed in an entirely different space-time, where people did not rush crossing the streets and no infant life was in danger, where everything turned away quite leisurely from the disaster.

In the hospital room, the box of cannoli still in my hand,

I saw Teri weeping over Isabel, who was deathly pale. Dr. Tomita was there, the images on the screen already pulled up and showing the hemorrhage in our daughter's head. It seemed that once the CSF drained, the tumor had expanded into the vacated space and its blood vessels started bursting. Immediate removal of the tumor was the only hope, but there was a distinct risk of Isabel's bleeding to death. A child of her age had no more than a pint of blood in her body, Dr. Tomita told us, and continuous transfusion might not suffice.

Before we followed Isabel into pre-op, I put the cannoli into the fridge in her room. The selfish lucidity of that act produced an immediate sense of guilt. Only later would I understand that absurd act as related to some form of desperate hope: the cannoli might be necessary for our future survival.

The surgery was to last four to six hours; Dr. Tomita's assistant would keep us updated. We kissed Isabel's parchment-pale forehead and watched her be wheeled into the unknown by a gang of masked strangers. Teri and I returned to the room to wait and see if our child would live through the night. We alternately wept and kept silent, always embraced. The assistant called us after a couple of hours, and said that Isabel was doing fine. We shared some cannoli, not to celebrate but to keep ourselves going—we'd had very little food and sleep. The lights in the room were dimmed; we were on a bed behind a curtain; for some reason, no one bothered us. We were far away from the world where there were farmer's markets and blueberries, where nurses changed shifts and gossiped, where other children were born and lived, where grandmothers put granddaughters to sleep. I had never felt as close to another human being as I did that night to my wife—transcendent love would be a plain way to describe what I felt.

Sometime after midnight, the assistant called to say that Isabel had made it through the surgery. We met Dr. Tomita outside the waiting room, in which some other unfortunate parents slept on uncomfortable sofas, coiled into their own nightmares. Dr. Tomita thought he'd removed most of the tumor; as luck would have it, the tumor did not burst, so blood did not flood the brain, which would've been lethal. Isabel did well and should be transferred to the Intensive Care Unit shortly, he said, where we could see her. I remember that moment as a relatively happy one: Isabel lived. Only the imminent outcome was relevant; all we could hope for was reaching the next step, whatever it was. The future was capped; there could be no life beyond Isabel's being alive *now*.

At the ICU, we found her entangled in a web of IV tubes and monitor wires, paralyzed by rocuronium (called "the rock" by everyone there), which had been given to prevent her from ripping out her breathing tubes. We spent the night watching her, kissing the fingers on her limp hand, reading or singing to her. The next day, I set up an iPod dock and played music, not only in a willfully delusional belief that music is good for a painful, recovering brain, but also to counter the soul-crushing hospital noise: the beeping of monitors, the wheezing of the breathing machinery, the indifferent chatter of nurses in the hallway, the siren that would go off whenever a patient's situation abruptly worsened. To the accompaniment of Bach cello concertos or Mingus piano pieces, my heart registered every dip of Isabel's heart rate, every change in her blood pressure. I couldn't take my eyes off the cruelly fluctuating numbers on the monitors, as though sheer staring could influence the outcome. All we could ever do was wait.

There's a psychological mechanism, I've come to believe, that prevents most of us from imagining the moment of our own death. For if it were possible to imagine fully that instant of passing from consciousness to nonexistence, with all the attendant fear and humiliation of absolute helplessness, it would be very hard to live, as it would be unbearably obvious that death is inscribed in everything that constitutes life, that any moment of our existence is a breath away from being the last one. We would be continuously devastated by the magnitude of that inescapable moment, so our minds wisely refuse to consider it. Still, as we mature into mortality, we gingerly dip our horror-tingling toes in the void, hoping that the mind will somehow ease itself into dying, that God or some other soothing opiate will remain available as we venture deeper into the darkness of nonbeing.

But how can you possibly ease yourself into the death of your child? For one thing, it is supposed to happen well after your own dissolution into nothingness. Your children are supposed to outlive you by several decades, in the course of which they'll live their lives, happily devoid of the burden of your presence, eventually completing the same mortal trajectory as their parents: oblivion, denial, fear, the end. They're supposed to handle their own mortality, and no help in that regard (other than forcing them to confront death by way of your dying) can come from you—death ain't a science project. And even if you could imagine your child's death, why would you?

But I'd been cursed with a compulsively catastrophic imagination, and had often involuntarily imagined the worst. I used to envision being run over by a car whenever I crossed the street, complete with a vision of the layers of dirt on the car's axle as its wheel crushed my skull. Or, stuck on a subway with all the lights out, I'd envision a deluge of fire advancing through the tunnel toward the train. Only after I met Teri did I manage to get my tormentful imagination under control. And after our children were born, I learned to quickly delete the visions of something horrible happening to them. A few weeks before Isabel's cancer was diagnosed, I'd noticed that her head was large and somewhat asymmetrical, and a question popped into my head: What if she has a brain tumor? But before my mind ran off with all the frightening possibilities, I talked myself out of considering them. She appeared to be in perfect health.

Even if you could imagine your child's grave illness, why would you?

A couple of days after Isabel's first resection, an MRI showed that there was a piece of tumor left in her brain. The more of the cancer taken out, the better her survival prognosis would be, so Isabel had to undergo another surgery, after which she returned to the ICU. Then, after she was transferred from the ICU to neurosurgery, her CSF was still not draining: an external ventricular drain (EVD) was put in, while a passage in her brain was surgically opened for drainage. She had fever again. The EVD was taken out; her ventricles became enlarged and full of fluid again, to the point of endangering her life; her blood pressure was dropping. Undergoing yet another emergency scan, facing upward in the MRI tunnel, she nearly choked, her vomit bubbling out of her mouth. Finally, a shunt was surgically implanted, allowing the CSF to drain directly into her stomach. In less than three weeks, Isabel had undergone two resections—whereby her cerebral hemispheres had to be parted to allow Dr. Tomita to access the region where the stem, the pineal gland, and the cerebellum meet, and scoop out the tumor—with six additional surgeries to address the failure of her CSF to drain. A tube had been inserted in her chest for administering chemotherapy drugs directly into her bloodstream. To top it all, an inoperable peanut-size tumor was detected in her frontal lobe, while the pathology report confirmed that the cancer was indeed ATRT. The chemo was set to start on August 17, a month after the diagnosis, and her oncologists, Dr. Fangusaro and Dr. Lulla, did not wish to discuss her prognosis. We did not dare press them.

During the first few weeks after Isabel's diagnosis, we did not eat or sleep much. Most of the time Teri and I were at the hospital, at Isabel's side. We tried to spend time with Ella, who was not allowed into the ICU, though she could visit Isabel in the neurosurgery ward, where she made Isabel smile every time they were together. Ella seemed to be handling the catastrophe pretty well. Supportive family and good friends came through our house, distracting her, helping us to cover up our continuous absence. When we talked to her about Isabel's illness, Ella listened, wide-eyed, concerned, and perplexed.

It was sometime in the first few weeks of the ordeal that Ella began talking about her imaginary brother. Suddenly, in an onslaught of her words we would discern stories about a brother who was sometimes a year old, sometimes in high school, and who would occasionally travel, for some obscure reason, to Seattle or California, only to return to Chicago to be featured in yet another adventurous monologue of Ella's.

It is not unusual, of course, for children of Ella's age to have imaginary friends or siblings. The creation of an imaginary character is related, I believe, to the explosion of the child's newly acquired linguistic ability, which occurs between the ages of two and four, and rapidly creates an excess of language that she may not have enough experience to match. The child has to construct imaginary narratives to try out the words she suddenly possesses. Ella now knew the word *California* but had no experience in any way related to it, nor could she conceptualize it in its abstract aspect, in its *Californianess*. Hence her imaginary brother had to be deployed to the sunny state, which allowed Ella to talk at length as if she knew California—the acquired words demanded the story, the language necessitated a fictional landscape. At the same time, the surge in language at this age creates a distinction between exteriority and interiority; the child's interiority is now expressible and thus possible to externalize; the world doubles. Ella could now talk about what was here and about what was elsewhere; the language made *here* and *elsewhere* continuous and simultaneous. Once, at our dinner table, I asked Ella what her brother was doing at that very moment. He was in her room, she said matter-of-factly, throwing a tantrum.

At first, her brother had no name, let alone a physical aspect. When asked what he was called, she'd respond, "Goo-goo Gaga," which was the nonsensical sound Malcolm, our five-year-old nephew and her favorite cousin, used when he didn't know the word for something. Since Charlie Mingus is practically a deity in our household, we suggested to Ella the name Mingus, and so Mingus her brother became. Soon thereafter, Malcolm gave her an inflatable doll of a space alien, which Ella subsequently elected to embody the existentially slippery Mingus. Though Ella would often play with her blown-up brother, the alien's physical presence was not always required for her to issue pseudoparental orders to Mingus, or tell a story of his escapades. While our world was being reduced to the claustrophobic size of ceaseless dread, Ella's world was expanding.

An atypical teratoid rhabdoid tumor is so rare that there are few chemotherapy protocols specifically designed for it, as it's very difficult to assemble a group of affected children big enough for a clinical trial. Many of the available protocols are derived from treatments for medulloblastomas and other brain tumors, modified with increased toxicity to counter the ATRT's vicious malignancy. Some of those protocols involve focused radiation treatment, but those would have significantly and detrimentally affected development in a child of Isabel's age. The protocol that Isabel's oncologists decided upon was of extremely high toxicity, consisting of six cycles of chemotherapy, the last one being the most intense. So much so, in fact, that Isabel's own immature blood cells, extracted earlier, would have to be reinjected after the last cycle, in a process called stem-cell recovery, to help her depleted bone marrow recover.

Throughout the chemo, she would also have to receive transfusions of platelets and red blood cells, while her white-blood-cell count would need to recover by itself each time. Her immune system would be temporarily annihilated, and, as soon as it recovered, another chemo cycle would begin. Because of her extensive brain surgeries, she could no longer sit or stand, and hence would have to undergo occupational and physical therapy, between the bouts of chemo. Sometime in the uncertain future, it was suggested, she might be able to return to the developmental stage expected of her age.

When her first chemo cycle began, Isabel was ten months old and weighed only sixteen pounds. On her good days she smiled heroically, more than any other child I've ever known, more than I ever will. Few though they may have been, the good days enabled us to project some kind of future for Isabel and our family: we scheduled her occupational and physical therapy appointments; we let our friends and family know what days would be good for visits; we put things down on the calendar for the upcoming couple of weeks. But the future was as precarious as Isabel's health, extending only to the next reasonably achievable stage: the end of the chemo cycle; the recovery of her white-blood-cell count; the few days before the next cycle when Isabel would be as close to being well as possible. I prevented my imagination from conjuring anything beyond that, refusing to consider either possible outcome of her illness. If I found myself envisioning holding her little hand as she was expiring, I would delete the vision, often startling Teri by saying aloud to myself: "No! No! No! No!" I blocked imagining the other outcome too—her successful survival—because some time ago, I'd come to believe that whatever I wanted to happen would not happen, precisely because I wanted it to happen. I'd therefore developed a mental strategy of eliminating any desire for good outcomes, as if my wishing would expose me to the hostile, spiteful forces that put up this ruthless universe. I dared not imagine Isabel's survival, because I thought I would thus jinx it.

Shortly after the start of Isabel's first chemo cycle, a well-intentioned friend of mine called and the first thing she asked was: "So, have things settled into some kind of routine?" Isabel's chemotherapy did, in fact, offer a seemingly predictable pattern. The chemo cycles had an inherent repetitive structure: the scheduled chemo drugs administered in the same order; the expected reactions: vomiting, loss of appetite, collapse of the immune system; the intravenous TPN (total parenteral nutrition) given because she was unable to eat; the antinausea drugs, antifungal drugs, and antibiotics administered at regular intervals; the expected transfusions; a few visits to the emergency room due to fever; the gradual recovery measured by rising blood counts; a few bright days at home. Then back in the hospital for a new cycle.

If Isabel and Teri, who seldom left her side, were in the hospital for the chemo, I'd spend the night at home with Ella, drop her off at school, then bring coffee and breakfast to my wife and, while she was having a shower, sing to or play with my daughter. I'd clean up Isabel's vomit or change her diapers, keeping them for the nurse so they could be weighed. In pseudoexpert lingo, Teri and I would discuss the previous night, what was expected that day; we'd wait for the rounds, so we could ask our difficult questions.

The human sense of comfort depends on repetitive, familiar actions—our minds and bodies strive to be accustomed to predictable circumstances. But no lasting routine could be established for Isabel. An illness such as ATRT causes a breakdown of all biological, emotional, and family routines, where nothing goes the way you expect it, let alone want it to. A day or two after the beginning of her TPN, while we were at home, Isabel unexpectedly went into anaphylactic shock, swelling rapidly and having trouble breathing, and so we rushed her to the emergency room. Besides the sudden catastrophic events, there was the daily hell: her coughing seldom ceased, which would often lead to vomiting; she'd have rashes and constipation; she'd be listless and weak; at the first sign of fever, we'd go to the ER; we could never tell her it would get better. No amount of repetition can get you used to that. The comfort of routines belonged to the world outside.

One early morning, driving to the hospital, I saw a number of able-bodied, energetic runners progressing along Fullerton Avenue toward the sunny lakefront, and I had an intensely physical sensation of being inside an aquarium: I could see outside, the people outside could see me inside (if they somehow chose to pay attention), but we lived and breathed in entirely different environments. Isabel's illness and our experience had little connection to, and even less impact on, the world outside. Teri and I were gathering undesirable, disheartening knowledge that had no application whatsoever in the outside world and was of no interest to anyone in it—the runners ran dully along into their betterment; people reveled in the stable banality of routine living; the torturer's horse kept scratching its innocent behind on a tree.

Isabel's ATRT made everything inside our life intensely, heavily real. Everything outside was not so much unreal as devoid of comprehensible substance. When people who didn't know about Isabel's illness asked me what was new, and I'd tell them, I'd witness their rapidly receding to the distant horizon of their own lives, where entirely different things mattered. After I told my tax accountant that Isabel was gravely ill, he said: "But you look good, and that's the most important thing!" The world sailing calmly on depended on the language of functional platitudes and clichés that had no logical or conceptual connection to our catastrophe.

I had a hard time talking to well-wishing people and an even harder time listening to them. They were kind and supportive, and Teri and I endured their babbling without begrudging it, as they simply didn't know what else to say. They protected themselves from what we were going through by limiting themselves to the manageable domain of vacuous, overworn language. But we were far more comfortable with the people wise enough not to venture into verbal support, and our closest friends knew that. We much preferred talking to Dr. Lulla or Dr. Fangusaro, who could help us understand things that mattered, to being told to "hang in there." (To which I would respond: "There is no other place to hang.") And we stayed away from anyone who, we feared, might offer us the solace of that supreme platitude, God. The hospital chaplain was prohibited from coming anywhere near us.

One of the most common platitudes we heard was that "words failed." But words were not failing Teri and me at all. It was not true that there was no way to describe our experience. Teri and I had plenty of language to talk to each other about the horror of what was happening, and talk we did. The words of Dr. Fangusaro and Dr. Lulla, always painfully pertinent, were not failing either. If there was a communication problem it was that there were too many words; they were far too heavy and too specific to be inflicted upon others. (Take Isabel's chemo drugs: vincristine, methotrexate, etoposide, cyclophosphamide, cisplatin—all creatures of a particularly malign demonology.) If something was failing it was the functionality of routine, platitudinous language—the comforting clichés were now inapplicable and perfectly useless. We instinctively protected other people from the knowledge we possessed; we let them think that words failed, because we knew they didn't want to be familiar with the vocabulary we used daily. We were sure they didn't want to know what we did; we didn't want to know it either.

There was no one else on the inside with us (and we certainly didn't wish anybody's children to have ATRT so we could talk to them about it). In "The Resource Guide for Parents of Children with Brain and Spinal Cord Tumors," which we were given to help us cope with our child's brain tumor, ATRT was "not discussed in detail" because it was too rare; in point of fact, it was entirely elided. We could not communicate even within the small group of families with children beset by cancer. The walls of the aquarium we were hanging in were made of other people's words.

Meanwhile, Mingus allowed Ella to practice and expand her language, while providing her with company and comfort Teri and I were barely able to provide. On the mornings when I drove her to school, Ella would offer run-on tales of Mingus, the recondite plots of which were sunk deep in her verbal torrent. Now and then, we'd witness her playing with Mingus—the alien or the fully imaginary one—administering fictional medicine or taking his temperature, using the vocabulary she had collected on her visits to the hospital, or from our talking about Isabel's illness. She'd tell us that Mingus had a tumor, was undergoing tests, but was going to get better in two weeks. Once Mingus even had a little sister named Isabel—entirely distinct from Ella's little sister—who also had a tumor and was, also, going to get better in two weeks. (Two weeks, I recognized, was just about the length of the future Teri and I could conceive of at the time.) Whatever accidental knowledge of Isabel's illness Ella was accumulating, whatever words she was picking up from participating in our experience, she was processing through her imaginary brother. She clearly missed her sister, so Mingus gave her some comfort in that respect as well. She longed for our being together as a family, which was perhaps why one day Mingus acquired his own set of parents and moved out with them to a place around the corner, only to return to us the next day. She externalized her complicated feelings by assigning them to Mingus, who then acted upon them.

One day at breakfast, while Ella ate her oatmeal and rambled on about her brother, I recognized in a humbling flash that she was doing exactly what I'd been doing as a writer all these years: in my books, fictional characters allowed me to understand what was hard for me to understand (which, so far, has been nearly everything). Much like Ella, I'd found myself with an excess of words, the wealth of which far exceeded the pathetic limits of my biography. I'd needed narrative space to extend myself into; I'd needed more lives; I, too, had needed another set of parents, and someone other than myself to throw my metaphysical tantrums. I'd cooked up those avatars in the soup of my ever-changing self, but they were not me—they did what I wouldn't or couldn't. Listening to Ella furiously and endlessly unfurl the yarns of the Mingus tales, I understood that the need to tell stories is deeply embedded in our minds, and inseparably entangled with the mechanisms that generate and absorb language. Narrative imagination—and therefore fiction—is a basic evolutionary tool of survival. We process the world by telling stories and produce human knowledge through our engagement with imagined selves.

Whatever knowledge I'd acquired in my middling fiction-writing career was of no value inside our ATRT aquarium, however. I could not write a story that would help me comprehend what was happening. Isabel's illness overrode any kind of imaginative involvement on my part. All I cared about was the hard reality of Isabel's breaths on my chest, the concreteness of her slipping into slumber as I sang my three lullabies. I did not wish or dare to imagine anything beyond her smiles and laughter, beyond her present torturous, but still beautiful, life.

Isabel received the last drug (cisplatin) of her third cycle on a Sunday afternoon in October. We were hoping she could go home on Monday morning, at least for a few days. Ella came to see her that same afternoon and, as always, made her laugh by pretending to grab little chunks of her cheeks and eat them. After Ella left, Isabel was agitated on my chest. I recognized a pattern in her restlessness: watching the second hand on the big clock in the room, I realized that she was twitching and whimpering every thirty seconds or so. Teri summoned the nurse, who talked to the oncologist on call, who talked to the neurologist, who talked to someone else. They thought she was having microseizures, but it was not clear why this was happening. Then she went into a full-blown seizure: she stiffened, her eyes rolled up, her mouth foamed while she kept twitching. Teri and I held her hands and talked to her, but she was not aware of us. Urgently, she was transferred to the ICU.

The names of all the drugs she was given and all the procedures she underwent in the ICU are obscure to me now, as is most of that night—what is hard to imagine is hard to remember. Isabel's sodium levels had precipitously dropped, which had caused the seizure; whatever they did to her stopped it. Eventually, breathing tubes were inserted and the rock was administered again. Isabel was going to stay in the ICU until her sodium levels stabilized.

But they never did. Though she came off the rock and the breathing tubes were taken out a couple of days later, she had to be constantly given sodium solution, at the expense of her TPN, without the levels ever returning to normal. On Halloween, while Teri was taking Ella trick-or-treating in our neighborhood, as had been promised, Isabel was restive again on my chest. The night before, which I'd spent at home with Ella, I'd had a dream in which Isabel was in my arms and then jerked violently back, as if in sudden pain, and I dropped her—I'd snapped out of the dream with a scream before she hit the ground. In the ICU room, I was desperately looping through the three lullabies, trying to calm her down. Even when she managed to fall asleep, I could feel her breathing stop only to start again, a frighteningly long moment later. The nurse on duty told me that sleep apnea was common in babies, and his obvious bullshit scared me more than it annoyed me. He informed the doctor on duty and what needed to be noted was duly noted. Soon thereafter, Teri and I switched, and I went home to be with Ella.

The phone rang in the middle of the night. Teri put Dr. Fangusaro on the phone to tell me that Isabel "had a really hard time" maintaining her blood pressure. I needed to come to the hospital as soon as possible.

Having dropped Ella off with my sister-in-law, I sped to the hospital. I found a crowd of the ICU staff outside Isabel's room looking inside, where Isabel was surrounded by a pack of doctors and nurses. She was bloated, her eyelids swollen. Her little hands were stabbed with needles, as liquid was pumped into her to keep her blood pressure up. Dr. Fangusaro and Dr. Lulla sat us down to tell us that Isabel's state was dire. Teri and I needed to tell them whether we would want them to try everything they could to save her. We said yes. They made it clear we would have to be the ones to tell them when to stop trying.

And now my memory collapses.

Teri is in the corner, weeping ceaselessly and quietly, the terror on her face literally unspeakable; the gray-haired attending doctor (whose name has vanished, though his face stares at me daily) is issuing orders as residents take turns compressing Isabel's chest because her heart has stopped beating. They bring her back, as I'm wailing: "My baby! My baby! My baby! . . ." Then there is another decision Teri and I have to make: Isabel's kidneys have stopped functioning; she needs dialysis and a surgical intervention on the spot is necessary to connect her to the dialysis machine—there is a good chance she might not survive the surgery. We say yes to it. Her heart stops beating again, the residents are compressing her chest. In the hallway outside, people unknown to me are rooting for Isabel, some of them in tears. "My baby! My baby! My baby! . . ." I keep howling. I hug Teri. Isabel's heart starts beating again. The gray-haired doctor turns to me and says, "Twelve minutes," and I cannot comprehend what he is saying. But then I realize: what he is saying is that Isabel was clinically dead for twelve minutes. Then her heart stops beating again, a young resident halfheartedly compressing her chest, waiting for us to tell her to stop. We tell her to stop. She stops.

In my eagerly, but not quickly enough, suppressed visions, I'd foreseen the moment of my child's death. But what I'd imagined against my best efforts was a quiet, filmic moment in which Teri and I held Isabel's hands as she peacefully expired. I could not have begun to imagine the intensity of the pain we felt as the nurses took out all the tubes and wires and everyone cleared out and Teri and I held our dead child— our beautiful, ever-smiling daughter, her body bloated with liquid and beaten by compressions—kissing her cheeks and toes. Though I recall that moment with absolute, crushing clarity, it is still unimaginable to me.

And how do you walk away from a moment like that? How do you leave your dead child behind and return to the vacant routines of whatever you might call your life? We put Isabel down on the bed, covered her with a sheet, signed whatever papers needed to be signed, packed all our stuff: her toys, our clothes, the iPod dock, the food containers, the debris of the before. Outside the room, somebody had put up a screen to give us privacy; all the good people who had rooted for Isabel were now gone. Carrying, like refugees, our large plastic bags full of stuff, we walked to the garage across the street, got into our car, and drove on the meaningless streets to my sister-in-law's.

I don't know what mental capacity is required for comprehending death—and I don't know at what age one acquires it, if ever—but Ella seemed to possess it. When we told her that her little sister had died, there was a moment of clear understanding on Ella's face. She started crying in a way that could only be described as unchildlike and said: "I want another little sister named Isabel." We're still parsing that statement.

Teri, Ella, and I—a family missing one—then went home. It was November 1, the Day of the Dead. A hundred and eight days had passed since Isabel's diagnosis.

One of the most despicable religious fallacies is that suffering is ennobling, that it is a step on the path to some kind of enlightenment or salvation. Isabel's suffering and death did nothing for her, or us, or the world. The only result of her suffering that matters is her death. We learned no lessons worth learning; we acquired no experience that could benefit anybody. And Isabel most certainly did not earn ascension to a better place, as there has never been a place better for her than Teri's breast, Ella's side, or my chest. Without Isabel, Teri and I were left with oceans of love we could no longer practice; we found ourselves with an excess of time we used to devote to her; we had to live inside a void that could be filled only by Isabel's presence. Isabel's indelible absence is now an organ in our bodies whose sole function is a continuous secretion of sorrow.

Ella talks about Isabel often. When she talks about her death she does so cogently, her words deeply felt; she knows what happened and what it all means; she is confronted by the same questions and longings as we are. Once, before falling asleep, she asked me: "Why did Isabel die?" Another time, she told me: "I don't want to die." Not so long ago, she started talking to Teri, out of the blue, about wanting to hold Isabel's hand again, about how much she missed Isabel's laughter. A few times, when we asked her if she missed Isabel, she refused to respond, exhibiting a kind of impatience that is entirely recognizable to us—what was there to talk about that was not self-evident?

Mingus is still good and well, going steadily about his alternative-existence business. Although he stays with us a lot, he lives around the corner yet again, with his parents and a variable number of siblings, most recently two brothers, Jackon and Cliff, and a sister, Piccadilly. He has had his own children—three sons, at one point, one of whom was called Andy. When we went skiing, Mingus preferred snowboarding. When we went to London for Christmas, Mingus went to Nebraska. He plays chess ("chest" in Ella's parlance) pretty well, it seems. Sometimes he yells at Ella ("Shut up, Mingus!" she yells back); other times he loses his own voice, but then speaks in Isabel's. He is also a good magician. With his magic wand, Ella says, he can make Isabel reappear.

TABLE OF DISCONTENTS

■ ■ ■

1. "The Lives of Others," first published as "The Other Questions" in *Der Andere Nebenan: The South-East-European Anthology*, ed. Richard Swartz, S. Fischer Verlag, Germany, 2007.
2. "Sound and Vision," first published as "To Catch a Thief" in *The Guardian Weekend*, July 10, 2004.
3. "Family Dining," originally published as two pieces: "Rationed," *The New Yorker*, September 3, 2007; and "Borscht," *The New Yorker*, November 22, 2010.
4. "The Kauders Case," *McSweeney's*, Issue 8, 2002.
5. "Life During Wartime," *The New Yorker*, June 12, 2006.
6. "The Magic Mountain," *The New Yorker*, June 8, 2009.
7. "Let There Be What Cannot Be," published as "Genocide's Epic Hero" in *The New York Times*, July 27, 2008.
8. "Dog Lives," first published as "War Dogs" in *Granta*, Issue 118, February 2012.
9. "The Book of My Life," *The New Yorker*, December 25, 2000.
10. "The Lives of a Flaneur," first published as "Mapping Home" in *The New Yorker*, December 5, 2011.
11. "Reasons Why I Do Not Wish to Leave Chicago: An Incomplete, Random List," first published in *Chicago in the Year 2000*, ed. Teri Boyd, 3 Book Publishing, 2006.

12. "If God Existed, He'd Be a Solid Midfielder," *Granta*, Issue 108, September 2009.
13. "The Lives of Grandmasters," unpublished.
14. "The Kennel Life," first published as "In the Doghouse" in *Playboy*, August 2006.
15. "The Aquarium," *The New Yorker*, June 13, 2011.

All the pieces were originally published in somewhat different form and have been revised and edited for this book.